BUYING HAPPINESS

Buying Happiness

BY EDGAR J. GOODSPEED

Essay Index Reprint Series

91938

BOOKS FOR LIBRARIES PRESS
FREEPORT, NEW YORK

First Published 1932
Reprinted 1968

LIBRARY OF CONGRESS CATALOG CARD NUMBER:

68-29207

PRINTED IN THE UNITED STATES OF AMERICA

To
ELFLEDA

PREFACE

Of the essays collected in this volume, six have appeared in the *Atlantic Monthly*, and three in the *Improvement Era*. The editors of these magazines have kindly given me permission to reprint these papers, and I am glad to acknowledge their kindness. One has reappeared in the *Reader's Digest*, and one, in a Spanish version, in *Inter-America*.

One was read at the dedication of the Henry M. Seymour Library at Knox College, and another at the dedication of the Tanner Memorial Library, at Illinois College, in connection with the celebration of the centennial of that institution. And one was presented—*impar congressus Achilli!*—before the Utah Academy of Arts and Letters, at a summer meeting, high among the passes of the Wasatch. So much for origins.

THE AUTHOR

CONTENTS

BUYING HAPPINESS

My pilgrim path sometimes takes me, whether I will or no, into the City of Destruction and among the enormous buildings of Vanity Fair. In their spacious and palatial interiors the air is soft and warm and sometimes even fragrant. A huge reception committee of affable young men and women occupies each building, so that you have but to express a wish for anything and simply for the mention of your name and address it is yours. A vast throng of happy people, mostly women, streams continually through the broad aisles of these great houses, which, wonderful to tell, stand wide open to the public from morning till evening, so that any may come in or go out, whether he have money or no.

Not less wonderful are the outsides of these houses, for, instead of walls, their sides are nothing but windows, until you marvel that the upper parts of them do not fall to the ground for want of support. These windows do not let light into the buildings, but each of them is boxed in like a little stage, set to be seen from the street; and, in truth, a great many spectators hurrying along the streets of the City of Destruction see these little scenes as they pass. Nor has any passer-by to pay any charge or fee for seeing them; he may even stop and look at them as long as he likes; none will turn him away.

Sometimes the scene is a stately old baronial hall with oaken wainscots and rich tapestries and huge ancient chairs like thrones. Sometimes it is a rich withdrawing room, with worldly men and women of wax, modishly dressed, ogling one another. But always the scene is rich and splendid. Never have I seen any poor or ragged man among these waxen actors, nor any ugly hovel among the scenes the little stages show.

The philosopher Epictetus remarks that a man who has good clothes and hangs them in the window to air should not lament if a thief comes by and appropriates them, since that would be to repeat the thief's mistake of supposing that to possess good clothes is in itself a good. And as I pass along our city streets, and steal at least a glance now and then at the show-windows elaborately set with exquisite ladies and sumptuous furniture, I am reminded of Epictetus. Back of all this cleverness in display, this seductive elegance, does there perhaps yet lurk some vestige, by implication at least, of the old mistake? Do not the gowns and furniture say in the clearest tones to our sight, "Possess us and be happy"?

I hasten to agree that these windows are, some of them, in the most excellent taste, that they are often a delight to the eye, and that they are, in many instances, historically correct in period and style. I cannot deny a certain educational value to them; they cultivate taste and contribute to intelligence. They undoubtedly afford pleasure to the passer-by, and relieve the inevitable dinginess and dulness of city streets with intervals of warmth, interest, and color. Of all the forms of advertising, they are perhaps the most reasonable and legitimate. Yet, after all, they certainly fall somewhat short of the moral ideal of Stoicism.

For what would Epictetus say to all this? Rather, what is the message of it all to the passer-by? Its message is, I suppose, "Stranger, enter in, and make these accessories of luxury yours by giving for them a fair return. These are such gowns as your wife and daughters should have; these are such rooms as they and you should live in; these are such chambers as real people retire to when the day is done. Such should be your surroundings. Such is life."

I doubt not many a man has gone home from viewing these refined splendors and removed an unworthy chromo from over the mantelpiece and many a woman has been led to strip the parlor furniture of tidies. Beyond question, they help to educate the public taste and raise the standard of living. And they probably interest many in actually buying something at least faintly resembling what they show. But it would be easy, under the influence of Epictetus, to exaggerate their seductive effect upon the seasoned citizen of the City of Destruction. He is a bird that has seen the net spread often enough before, and it is his art to take the bait and leave the hook. He knows "The Fable of the Married Pair Who Were Ruined by Being Given a Grand Piano." His first emotion on beholding the rich and massive furniture of a baronial hall is joy that he does not have to pay the hall rent. A snug apartment where you can sleep on a door and eat in a cupboard is about his size, and a couple of footstools would be all the baronial furniture he could accommodate.

This great emancipation from the accumulations of furniture which our ancestors, baronial or other, thought necessary of course leaves a better market for the other merchandise the windows offer, such as dresses. The succinct style of these, so suited to the spirit of the age, is entirely compatible with the narrow limits of the modern abode. It no longer takes an armory or an aresenal to accommodate our wardrobes, as in the days when ladies wore hoops and gentlemen hardware.

It should surprise no one, therefore, if the habiliments of fashion thus seductively displayed lure the seasoned shopper into the fatal web. What does occasion surprise is the dismay with which even this partial success fills its contrivers. Only today I was stirred by the distress of two great store-managers who found their employees buying silk stockings to wear at labor. The Walrus and the Carpenter! After agonizing efforts to advertise silk stockings, after wonderful window displays of fashionable ladies wearing them, how disconcerting to find the public actually and extravagantly buying and paying for the very articles the managers have been moving heaven and earth to sell them! Who would not weep? Did not Alexander weep when he succeeded in what he undertook? He did. They do.

Nothing is more entertaining than the horror of the rich at the extravagance of the poor. Having exhausted ingenuity and sacrificed health to get what they call a "market" for their goods, they are shocked to find common people wearing them. But if it be wrong for the poor to wear such things, why does all business conspire to get them to buy? Why are they pursued all the time and everywhere with adjurations to do so? What is there to see in a modern city but the show-windows and the signs? Of course, the philosophic mind will find the library and the museum, where advertising has not yet penetrated; but everywhere on the street and in the cars the business of buying is eternally thrust upon you in season and out of season until it seems as though there were nothing else to think about.

I would not deride the genuine solicitude sometimes felt by the affluent for the more diligent members of society, nor forget their well-meaning efforts to guide us in the narrow path to honorable wealth. Under a frugal impulse I recently established a small savings account, as promising a possibly painless way of providing against a subscription I had been weak enough to make. What was my happiness to receive this flattering evidence that my obscure hoard had gained the approbation of the banking fraternity; and not unnaturally, for had I but invested it, as I thought of doing (and as my banker doubtless has done), it would have made me 50 per cent instead of 3. But hear his gracious words:

"Persistence in the accumulation of money will make it easier to do the things that you may later wish to do. Your first deposit is only the first step. The first thousand dollars will be great progress. Once beyond that and you will be well on the way to being the master of your financial situation."

Would that I would! But alas! The vice-president has not sufficiently explored my financial situation. It will take more than the first thousand to set me well on the way. Bankers should be less sanguine and optimistic about money matters, and not so carried away by rhetorical impulses. At the mere thought of three ciphers they lose their heads. This one is right in perceiving that I want encouragement, but not at such extravagant cost. From a banker, at all events, what one desires is not rainbows, but the truth.

Nor are the bankers—jolly fellows!—the only ones ready to help us on our upward way. Having a young friend with leanings toward the chauffeur's calling, I recently wrote to an automobile college for a catalogue, which promptly came. It was followed by a letter which, in the face of native incapacity and previous engagements, almost swept me into that profession. Like the banker, the college president was all hope.

"There is a big future ahead of you," he boldly wrote, "if you will only prepare for it now. The vital point of interest to you right now is: 'Will you be too old to enjoy your success when it comes and *if* it does come.' Let me answer that question for you. You will not be too old for this enjoyment if you determine to start right now on the road to success. The gate to success is my shops. In a period of only eight short weeks you can master the training and be able to step out into the world and be a man among men, have the necessaries and luxuries of life, and be a credit to yourself and to your loved ones. The thing for you to do, Mr. Goodspeed, is to decide now to jump on the next car bound for the shops and tell the world that you are headed for success and no one can stop you."

If only I had received this stirring letter earlier in life, everything might have been different.

Window-dressing, I own, sometimes takes extreme forms. When Tutankhamen was in flower, an original spirit in the drygoods business asked of me the loan of a mummy from the museum for a few days to give a lifelike touch to an Egyptian scene. I would set no limits to the window-dresser's art, but surely this verged on the impractical. What profit to create a craving for mummies in the passer-by? Thus is the human spirit, caught in the strong currents of enthusiasm, carried past its goal.

For my part I enjoy show-windows, and I approve of them. They brighten the way about the otherwise dismal streets of the City of Destruction. And to the men who have provided them I am grateful. But I am prepared to take

9

the consequences, and to acquiesce in the purchase of their contents by persons something
less than baronial in station. If they can pay,
let them buy, say I. If it be unwise, only thus
will they learn so. But, wise or foolish, they
are getting what they are paying for, which is
satisfaction.

The school teachers of the City of Destruction
having recently been granted a slight increase
in wages, politely known as "salary," a loud
outcry was raised, not at the increase, but because they spent it, it was said, "like drunken
sailors," on their personal adornment. What a
boon it is that we can thus derive pleasure from
condemning one another's purchases, and all
absolutely without cost to ourselves. The rich
perceive that the poor are improvident; the
poor consider the rich extravagant; the employer laments the prodigality of his employees; the
banker grieves over the luxury of the farmer;
the politician agonizes over the school teachers
spending their increase like drunken sailors.
Broadly speaking, the spenders are evidently all
wrong—or all right.

What most of these critics of expenditure fail
to see is that it is not economic, but psychologi-

cal, needs that these spenders, poor as well as rich, are meeting. They are buying something more than food and clothes. They are buying pleasure, enjoyment, happiness. It would be a drab world if they could not and did not.

I could wish that these critics might visit, as I have done, lands where people are not concerned to go beautifully. I would have them not simply pass through on a train, but get off and live there, month after month, for a year, seeing perhaps one or two well-dressed people a week. I would guarantee in them at the end such a state of mental depression at the sheer sordid unloveliness of their human horizon as might disturb even their economic pessimism, and make them see a little deeper into this business of buying and selling, which after all is not the whole of life.

Some people, to begin with, find a genuine pleasure in buying. What they buy may also be useful to them afterward. It may even be very useful. It may be worth far more than it cost. But over and above all this there is an insubstantial return they have received in the enjoyment of buying it. Nor is this an unreal thing, unless it be supposed that all merely pleasurable emotions are unreal. They certainly function really enough in this business of buying and selling, as the very pleasant places in which we are invited to buy clearly show.

Nor need it be thought that this pleasure in the sheer buying is a merely momentary satisfaction. It is rather the culmination of an extended social process known as shopping and often maligned by the uninformed. In this enjoyable process, and in the overt act of purchase in which it culminates, reside real if imponderable values with which any understanding economic estimate must reckon.

An opulent traveler once overwhelmed his fellow-tourists by making them costly presents from the lands they visited. To their protestations he replied that he enjoyed buying such things but really had no use for them afterward. More people are like that than realize it. It is a wise man who understands himself.

Here belongs the economically indefensible practice of "collecting." Experienced collectors have been known to express the hope that their heirs would sell their collections, in order to begin others of their own, since the joy lies in making the collection, not in possessing it.

BUYING HAPPINESS

This should be remembered before indulging in superficial criticism of the Shah of Persia for collecting clocks, or the Esquimaux for collecting alarm clocks. It is the act of acquisition that enthralls.

Beyond doubt the buyings of many of us look strange to most. One man buys first editions, all the dearer if uncut; another, Lincoln manuscripts, not to publish—that would spoil their value—but to protect from publication; another, bindings, regardless of what they contain; another, Chinese snuffboxes, though he is not Chinese and does not take snuff. "Cui bono?" says the sensible man to all this.

"Multo bono," I would reply. They are all buying the same thing in different packages. They are buying happiness.

THE ART OF BEING OUTSHONE

SOMEBODY is forever sending me literature about how to shine at dinners and in the social circle generally. It seems there are books full of anecdotes, repartees, and bright remarks, which, if memorized and opportunely remembered, are supposed to enliven these occasions. The master of these books dazzles and entertains every circle he enters. He holds the spotlight and the center of the stage. Murmurs of admiration attend his brilliant sallies. He is, in short, the life of the party.

Others, it appears, just as good as he, go home depressed and disheartened. They have not shone. The spotlight has not rested well pleased upon them. They have been obscure. Sound cause for gloom! Their minds, destitute of the thousand epigrams of the master spirits of the ages, have contributed nothing brilliant to the conversation.

It is evident from the amount and tone of this literature that one must shine to be happy. Without shining life is not worth while. One is

14

a failure, and might as well give up. It is the obviousness of this truth that provides a public for the literature. People have, indeed, often felt the sense of discouragement these circulars describe, and are glad to find a promise of relief, even though at the fateful moment they fumble in memory for the bright saying of Marcus Aurelius or Mark Twain which the occasion so pressingly demands. Perhaps, after all, it may be more practical to go to a dinner with just one bright but borrowed remark stored up for the occasion, and, watching narrowly your opportunity, to hurl that, like Bruce's heart, into the fray, than to carry in such a sackful of anecdotes gathered at random from five hundred minds.

There is, of course, nothing new about this yearning for notice and conspicuousness. It is an inheritance from childhood and even from antiquity. Epictetus discussed it. It is hard, he admits, to hear another man discoursing brightly on a subject beyond your depth, and on which you have nothing to say. But courage! Another time the talk will be of grammar, and it will be your turn to shine.

The illuminating thing about this is that the

fine old Stoic himself was not above the common desire to shine, only he had sense enough to see that no sensible person expects or wishes to do all the shining. Every dog is entitled to his day—that is, of course, if he can get it. I do not say he would have ordered the books advertised above; he knew he needed no such meretricious aids to luminosity, being convinced that, taking the season together, he and every other well-disciplined philosopher were sure in due time to get their conversational innings. But he was evidently strongly disposed to have those innings soon or late.

It is odd that it did not occur to the ancient Stoic or the modern Epicurean that the true solution of the problem, which is evidently so vital to them, is the cultivation of the art of transition. To the master of transition, it matters not whether the talk be of the Taj Mahal or of the composition of rubber. Give him but the suspicion of a lull in the conversation and he will with a mere phrase bring it round to port.

Only last night on the way into the dining-room I heard an accomplished converser lamenting the general lack of interest in Africa—

one of his best themes. What weakness! Let him but contrive a set of good transitions, and I'll warrant he can bring the talk back to Africa though it have strayed as far afield as the nebula of Andromeda or the Great Hereafter. As thus: "How different that is from Africa, now!" or "You don't say so! Well, I remember once in Africa . . . ."

Of course, we all know the conversational superman; he has been with us since boyhood, to which period of development he properly belongs. He is always capping your modest contributions with something bigger. If you have slain your thousands, he has slain his tens of thousands. You timidly intimate that your assessed valuation is two thousand dollars; he cries that his is four. You say that you are to speak in Freeport; he says that they had previously asked him. You tell how long it took to drive a certain route; his time was better by hours. It does not matter that you happen later to detect much exaggeration in these quick rejoinders—as that his assessment is only about half yours. The mischief is done, or, rather, the success achieved. For evidently the skill of the thing lay in thinking quickly of the better

17

story and putting it over convincingly. It is not a matter of fact, but of art.

Such men are not liars. They are great hearty boys who have never learned the art of being outshone. Their fish are always bigger, their scores lower, their losses greater, their winnings larger, their operations dreadfuler, than yours. They have no need of the thousand best epigrams of the world's five hundred brightest minds, nor need they, like Epictetus, wait for another day when the talk is of grammar in order to shine. Their simple art is to snatch a reflected glory from every other's remark and multiply it thirty, sixty, a hundred fold.

What a good thing it is that there are no such women! Yet this may seem to have an ungracious ring; which reminds us: Let us now praise gracious women, the noble army of hostesses and dinner partners who listen patiently and with interest marvelously sustained —or simulated—to your interminable anecdotes and expositions, which are often no better than the thousand best efforts of the world's master minds, to say the least. Surely if there be pretense in this, the Recording Angel, if he must jot it down, will never be better occupied than in dropping some of his tears upon the page.

I have just had a delightful interview with a charming old gentleman. I enjoyed it exceedingly, but as I look back upon it two or three things emerge like islands from a sea. He was, it appeared, the best student and the best speaker his ancient college had ever produced, and to this day his record has not been surpassed. He next formed the laudable ambition of making himself the best preacher in the country, and, from all I can gather, he made decided progress in that direction. But I am fearful that he has never progressed far in the gentler art of being outshone.

A distinguished editor, on being asked on what principle he chose the articles that he printed, said that if a thing was so absorbing that a man would stop eating his roast beef to listen to it, he thought it worth publishing. No fairer description of prandial achievement can well be framed. And yet, with hundreds of thousands of copies of the select epigrams of the master minds flying about and equipping the most ordinary people overnight to hold dinner tables spellbound, even the roast-beef test may fail. To have the art, literature, history, politics, and business of the world on the tip of your tongue (What a tongue, to have such a tip!) may deceive even the elect into supposing that you know something about them. Better not make any pauses—except for the inevitable murmurs of admiration, which, it seems, are guaranteed—else some dull, malicious fellow may ask a disconcerting question. Still, not if he is spellbound; the thing is unthinkable. But for safety's sake a good dashing transition should always be taken along, as a kind of conversational parachute, in case your gas fails.

I have long been thinking that our artists should be painting scenes in real life, such as an automobile salesman and his prey. But whose pencil could portray the dinner table at which two accomplished possessors of the thousand epigrams of the master spirits should meet? The imagination reels at the picture. Gastronomically, the dinner would of course be a failure, for no one would have a moment's attention to give the food. One would inevitably get the jump upon the other at the start, and then, pausing presently for the inevitable murmur of admiration, would be dismayed to hear the other strike in with some apposite observation of Josh Billings or Hippocrates, and feel the spotlight fading from his brow. Can he regain it? His adversary is forewarned by now, and, if he knows his stuff, will give him no further chance, but rather a much-needed lesson in the Art of Being Outshone.

This "hyperlampophobia," or dread of being outshone, has begun to affect literature. Where is the so-called hero of yore? In many a modern tale the hero is really the simplest, fondest, most blundering being in the whole cast. Is it not clear that the old-style smart individual who easily gets his own way in all circumstances—an obvious aristocratic type—is out of date? The modern hero does not command your homage; he appeals to your compassion. You perceive that the poor fellow needs help, and how you long to be at his side and warn and cheer him, as, helpless with horror, you behold him blindly plunging deeper and deeper into difficulties. Only when his situation has become absolutely irremediable does the author let up on him. All this, of course, is for your good, so that you may not feel yourself too palpably outshone.

Take the old detective story. All was hopelessly obscure until the great detective entered. It presented no particular difficulties to him. A few blood drops, cigarette stubs, or bits of tweed, and the thing was done, all by himself. But nowadays there is a whole school of detective literature from which the detective hero has actually disappeared! He has simply vanished, leaving no trace. The truth is, we have grown tired of the omniscient detective who finds everything so easy, and prefer to see difficulties more democratically unraveled by a number of people, each contributing his bit and making the solution a social process.

Modern publicity methods have long since accustomed us to having our failings of every kind familiarly assumed and played upon, and we do not so much mind this unless our moral characters are impugned. Thus the frank challenge, "Why let Blunders in speech and writing put you at a Disadvantage? Beware of shabby English! Errors in Pronunciation can ruin the whole Effect of what you say!" while perhaps unconventional, does not offend us. Our Eng-

lish may be blundersome, shabby, and mispro-
nounced, as the advertiser so calmly assumes,
but if it is a bit informal at times, it is our own
business, no doubt. But to approach us on the
cool supposition that we go home from a party
unhappy if we have not done all the talking is
a different matter, and seems to assume that
we are all indeed but children of a larger
growth, if even that. To monopolize conversation is a thing no civilized man should ever
want to do.

Psychologists suggest that it is really better
for our mental health to do a good deal of
listening, claiming that in this way we may
get some of the stimulus and intellectual pabu-
lum that our spirits require. Experienced
diners-out, with a large and quick turnover, will
certainly confirm this, telling tonight the best
things they heard last night, but keeping silent
long enough to pick up a few new trifles for
tomorrow, when they sincerely hope to en-
counter a new circle of guests to try them on.

Such is, we believe, the democratic way of
life, but it is not that of the conversational
crammers, on the one hand, or of Epictetus, on
the other. They both aim at a larger but slower

business; at least Epictetus did. This was his professorial bent: unhappy except when lecturing; an evident stranger to the joyful activity of the intercreative mind. But how much better, really, to match wits with some capable table companion, until some new phase of common experience or interpretation emerges, to the general joy! A far better thing this than lecturing each other alternate evenings, you tonight, I tomorrow night! Little genius in such division of labor.

For what we are here concerned with is of course nothing less than the art of conversation. How many a man who thinks he is talking well, if lengthily, has really been launched and steered upon his course by the unobtrusive skill of his neighbor at table, who listens with apparent delight as he details the exploits of his lifelong hero:

"I said, 'Stand up; tell your story.' He did. I said, 'Sit down. Now tell yours.' She did. I said, 'You were right; he was wrong,' " and so on.

Such people are doomed to starvation, psychologists declare. They merely recite their little Odyssey until they are exhausted, and when rested up recite it over again, never giving themselves any chance to take in new ideas. It is perhaps comforting to reflect upon this righteous law of conversational compensations; and yet it is too often we rather than they who suffer the direct effects of their famine.

I am not exactly a hermit. To me the most interesting thing about this world through which I am passing is the people who live in it. They are also the most amusing thing in it. This is the heart of humanism—the world of personality over against the material world. The latter sometimes seems to engross us, and it is heresy to depreciate it. But, vast as it is, I sometimes wonder if it is any more stupendous than a great man's idea of it. Wonderful as it is, is it any more wonderful than that he can form and carry in his mind an image, however imperfect, of it? Yet he is but one of millions, every one of whom forms and carries such an image—material, social, moral, economic. Every person carries a world about with him of his own creation, or, at least, discovery. None of these images is wholly true, yet every one of them possesses some truth. No two of them are alike; perhaps no two of them should be alike. They are of an inexhaustible variety of attitude, opinion, information. It is a mistake to suppose that only the intelligent have definite opinions; the most definite opinions are held by the unintelligent, and they also hold them most strongly.

It is this that literature seeks to mirror, catching perhaps a hundred-millionth part, the best or worst, and "reducing it to writing," as we rightly say—for how much it is reduced! Which is what gives to literature such interest and glory as it possesses. But the thing itself is vastly greater than any record or even experience—not to say fancy—of it.

You see a man coming up the street, a person perhaps of little social, political, or financial standing. None the less, he carries about with him a private individual universe, as definite as your own, and in some parts, at least, sounder than yours. In it he alone is judge; his estimates and opinions prevail. You yourself are to him but a part of it, and subject to his verdicts and appraisals. If he is informed, capable, and wise, his ideas will be sounder; but many an ignorant and prejudiced person, if he be reflective and kind, carries about a universe well worth knowing.

Everybody is, in short, a kind of peripatetic Atlas bearing a world upon his shoulders. More than a world—a universe. It is no great flight of fancy to imagine the city streets filled with people so occupied. Yet most of them give no sign of finding the task burdensome. They are more like people carrying balloons. This is certainly a better figure, for if some are weighed down with the weight of their universe, others are plainly buoyed up by theirs. These balloons are of very different sizes, so that while one is hardly visible, another fills the whole sky. But, you will say, this means endless collisions between rival universes. And of course that is precisely what is constantly taking place, unless one knows how to handle his private universe with good taste and good manners. It is like the conflict of umbrellas on a crowded street on a rainy day, only on a much grander and more serious scale. The balloons are also of very different densities, and of different colors—black, blue, gray, brown, rose, yellow, purple, and orange. Everyone is very sensitive about his own particular one; nobody likes to have any liberties taken with his universe. And how fortunate it is that they are really or nearly invisible! Otherwise we should all be too often and too palpably outshone.

A CANDLE FOR SAINT BONIFACE

MUCH going to and fro in the earth and walking up and down therein have bred in me if not perpetual at least occasional benediction. The object of this gratitude is a figure little celebrated in modern liturgies, whom I venture to canonize as Saint Boniface. Not, of course, the well-known martyr of that name who evangelized Germany, though in my adventurous youth I have found comfort in many a German inn. Nor that jovial pope who, all unconscious of prohibition, promised indulgence to all good fellows who should ever drink his health. Precise hagiologists, indeed, will pompously declare my Boniface no saint at all, but a mere figment of modern fiction.

This puny origin is, I submit, an utterly unworthy and unsatisfying one for the eponym of universal hospitality. If such an order have not a patron saint, who of us should? Have not hunters Saint Hubert? And Democrats Saint Tammany, though they make little of his honors, being content to relate that he was a very, very good Indian, the wise chief of the Lenni-Lenape? But I can bear witness to his sainthood, for I have been in his parish, dined at his hotel, and traveled on the good ship that bears his name.

I therefore invite all travelers, which is to say everybody, to join me in offering saintly honors to Boniface. And I now place my slender taper before his modest shrine. It is, in short, the modern hotel keeper—or, more exactly, the keeper of the modern hotel—whom I would celebrate. He shall be my muse supreme, and light and lead me to my theme.

Bigger things than candles have been offered to Saint Boniface before now, and those who rate saints by the size of the offerings made to them may well take note of this. For, in a beautiful village I wot of, a man has erected and actually endowed a delightful hotel, richly furnished within, and without—*pace* Saint Andrew!—equipped with a golf course all its own. Myself, as a devotee of Saint Boniface, I see in this incident everything to admire, and rate the donor above the givers of libraries and playgrounds, if not of hospitals and schools. Would that every successful son of an inhospitable town might thus ennoble his native place, endowing it with the perfect grace of hospitality! Surely generations of pilgrims would rise up to call him blessed.

And if the hotel be the index of civilization, what better thing can one do than to build a good one and set the index forward, thus giving civilization something to overtake? But this is hardly a fair way of putting it, either. For who has not motored up a broad, shady street, bordered with stately houses, where people dwell in comfort and at ease, only to find that the place has no spot fit to eat in, to say nothing of sleeping?

Which brings me to the heart of the matter, and the real cause of my unfeigned gratitude to Saint Boniface. For it has suddenly occurred to me that the wonder and marvel of it all is that in a place I never heard of till yesterday Boniface has been for years prepared for my reception and comfort, and has been, as it were, waiting for me.

Of course, not for me alone; but none the less really ready and waiting for me. And if I stay away a generation and then go there again he will once more be ready and waiting. Ready at the Rhone Glacier, just beyond the summit of the Furca Pass, if you please; and ready at the Beaurivage in Geneva, where you stopped once thirty years ago, and where our patient Boniface has been taking down the shutters and opening the *salle à manger* every day these thirty years and more, in readiness for your return. Surely there is something saintly in all this. It is nothing less than the perseverance of the saints, and has something of the sublime regularity of nature itself, by virtue of which, while the earth remaineth, summer and winter and day and night shall not cease.

And if, sometimes, prices seem a trifle in excess of what we could buy and cook the breakfast for ourselves, we must remember that it is only fair to pay something toward all the preparations that have been at our service and steadily waiting our convenience all the times we have not been here. But this may be a dangerous suggestion to offer to the order of Saint Boniface, and I will not pursue it.

If the age and size of his shrines be criteria, the architecture of Boniface will hold its own with the best of them. The Crown at Slough is centuries older than Saint Peter's, and who does not know that the largest dome in the world is part of a hotel at West Baden, Indiana? And if it comes to atmosphere, what are Karnak and Stonehenge to the decayed but mighty splendors of Saratoga Springs?

That Boniface is a creation of English fiction is, I submit, an idea decisively negatived by his English style. Indeed, the extraordinary possibilities of our noble English tongue remain quite unexplored by the stay-at-home element of our population. The stateliest of Madrid hotels has its floors obligingly numbered 1th, 2th, 3th, and so on, a sight to cheer the elevator rider even in the warmest weather. "Please not expel any cigarettes and no matches to the windows," plaintively pleads the Métropole Suisse in Como. Could the thing be more engagingly and disarmingly presented? It is simply impossible to take offense.

This restraint of expression surely reaches its climax at Ivrea, as you come down the valley from the Great St. Bernard Pass, where you have just paid your respects to the famous stuffed life-saver in the convent parlor. At Ivrea you read without surprise, "Client has not to draw dogs into his room or into restaurant."

What a relief! Clearly you might have had to. But you do not. By the mercy of Saint Boniface you can retire peacefully to rest without having to draw dogs anywhere.

Perhaps you have never drawn a dog, and hardly know how to begin. Of course, dogs do draw travelers; A traveler by the faithful hound Half buried in the snow was found, and it may be necessary in some circumstances for the traveler, acting as the animal's client, to return the compliment. But why into the restaurant? If it is what it should be, it should not be necessary to draw the dog within. The thing is full of problems. And what a relief it is, this first day in many years on Italian soil, to know that, weary as you are with the long ride from Territet over the pass and down that glorious valley, you need not attempt the feat tonight.

Then, too, there is a positively pastoral solicitude about the modern Boniface. The precautions he takes against losing us by fire are an example. There is always the primitive method of leaving under the bed a long rope, made fast to the bedpost. The operation of this device is, of course, obvious. You simply seize the loose end firmly in both hands and jump from the window. Far more enjoyable is the coiled-spring contrivance sometimes seen in resort hotels. The directions instruct you to seat yourself upon the crossbar and slip lightly from the window sill to the ground. There was to be a fire drill the day after we left the Grand Canyon Hotel, and it was a bitter disappointment to me not to remain and see the guests gracefully parachuting from their several windows to the ground, and then, presumably, sailing lightly up again, as the powerful spring reasserted itself. Strange that no hotel has thought to advertise itself with a picture of this commanding spectacle, so appealing to the timid and the adventurous alike.

Of course it goes without saying that one must not approach Boniface empty-handed. Besides the check book, one will often need a set of tools and some simple practical devices such as wedges to stop the windows rattling, some black cloth to suspend before them to keep out the intermittent electric signs which are found in the more barbarous settlements, perhaps a nail or two to hang the shaving mirror on, and a small can of thick black paint to smear over the transom to keep the hall light out. A British guide earnestly advises visitors to France to take along a brick to place on the heater in the car floor to keep their feet from being burned. But far more essential is a set of football pads to be worn in scrambling on French trains, when all the reckless daring of the Gallic bourgeoisie appears in full flood.

But fashions change, and Boniface is getting so fastidious and exclusive about his votaries that I am resolved before visiting his foreign shrines again to provide myself with a rubber stamp declaring my name, age, rank, religion, politics, nationality, nativity, parentage, matrimonial state, purpose in life, and the like, so that I may not have to stand at his portal trying to remember and set down these particulars before being shown a place to lay my head. Especially when physically wearied after a long day's ride, and mentally exhausted with trying to remember all the various Louis's and Philips, and their miscellaneous womankind, and what (if anything) each was noted for, it is tedious to have to write out where you spent last night, and where you mean to spend the next one, when you landed and what you are doing here anyway, besides answering ingenious questions which you never thought of before, the answers to which cannot possibly be of any value or even interest to anyone in the world. What do they do with all these materials afterward, one wonders. Have you and I really our respective dossiers in the Sûreté and Scotland Yard, or the Home Office? And if my purpose in life underwent a change in the course of my travels, and was duly so reported, would it matter very much to them, and what would they do about it?

It is surely saintly business to rouse us, as Boniface does, to frenzies of benevolence or iconoclasm; to raise us to heights of crusading enthusiasm or plunge us into depths of asceticism. An American gentleman at Tours last summer was ruefully regarding the well-known frugal Continental breakfast set before him. Questioned as to his state of mind, he reported unfavorably. He said he had slept between two damp sails, with a rock for a pillow. What does asceticism require of its votaries more than this?

And as for ecstasies of benevolence, who has not felt the swelling inner impulse to bestow all the residue of his estate to provide bathrooms for England or sanitation for France? The sewers of Paris, I have come to fear after touring the French provinces, owe their fame chiefly to the fact that they were apparently the only ones Victor Hugo knew.

As for a crusade of iconoclasm, have you never felt a burning zeal to go through the inns and hostelries of England with axe and hammer, breaking in pieces the ponderous Victorian washbowls and pitchers that still fill the land, to make room for the running hot and cold water of today? What a glorious smash they would make, too—always an important point with iconoclasts.

In the pleasant land of France, last summer, a sock failed to come back from the wash. The chambermaid investigated and with infinite regret made her report: The *chaussette* of Monsieur had fallen into the water! Fatal fall, in France, where, as French writers faithfully inform us, labor is not dully standardized as here, but the washer-woman kneels gayly on the river bank and blithely washes the clothes in ice water. Truly a short life, but a merry one.

In the south of England, so entrancingly

beautiful (in fine weather), there is still shown the spot where once stood an inn in which Dr. Samuel Johnson descanted to Mr. James Boswell on the felicity of England in the possession of her inns and taverns. That was long ago, of course, and it must be admitted that the posture of things has somewhat altered. Few of us would today pitch upon this particular point for especial dilation, though Mr. J. S. Fletcher still utters an occasional chirp of satisfaction over it. Beyond question, points of view differ. Thus it does not allure me to read upon the sign of the Old Crown Hotel, at Slough, that it was established in 1315. It may indeed still offer all the comforts of the Middle Ages, but I had rather stay the night in one established in 1915—if such there be.

Yet I must insist that the best of all motor guides, in prefacing its list of British hotels with Christina Rossetti's poem on Death, while undoubtedly headed in the right general direction, goes too far:

> Will there be beds for me and all who seek?
> Yea, beds for all who come.

If I understand Miss Rossetti, she is not here speaking of hotel accommodations, although a hasty reader might gain that impression. On the other hand, I cannot believe that the genial Mr. Dunlop intended this as a malicious fling at the British hotel industry, of which, as we have seen, Englishmen have been loud in their praises at least from the days of Samuel Johnson. I prefer to see in the incident one of those subtle exhibitions of sturdy British humor, which are, alas! too often lost upon our untraveled fellow-countrymen.

THE AGE OF SALESMANSHIP

Ours is the Age of Salesmanship.

Not the Age of Steam, nor Steel, nor Electricity, nor Gasoline, as some have superficially assumed. These are mere externals. Not the Age of Reason, nor of Democracy, nor of Law. Not even the Age of Youth, though Youth is just now the universal vogue.

But what would Youth be without Salesmanship to give it direction and meaning? Standing with uncertain feet, Youth hears the trumpet call of Salesmanship, telling it what to eat, drink, chew, smoke, wear, see, hear, and take. The mind cannot be vacant nor the will inactive in such an age. For obviously when all the wayside thunders at you the imperious challenge, "Eat Raisins! Every Wednesday is Raisin Day!" you cannot remain neutral. Either worn down by successive avalanches of Salesmanship you will feebly murmur, "I will! I will," or summoning your last ounce of resistance for one final effort, you mutter through set teeth, "It's not! I won't!"

41

It is useless to deny the important shaping effect the tide of Salesmanship is having upon the modern mind. All that is in doubt is what shape the mind will take under its influence. When every mossy old barn along the highway tenderly murmurs "Chew Red Man, the Mild Mellow Chew," shall we yield to the alluring picture it subtly conjures up, or, repelled by its cannibalistic implications, shall we resolutely close our minds to the invitation?

The illustration may seem unimportant, yet our future as a people hangs in a sense upon the issue. Are we to be a race of weaklings, amenable to every advance of Salesmanship, or a generation of Spartans, bold enough to say No?

"Buy British Goods—British and Best," sturdily counsels the cover page of a well-known English quarterly. The solid candor of this appeal, so wholly free from self-consciousness or timidity, must at least command our admiration, even though its psychology is not our own. The clamors of the Canadian landscape that we "Drink Blotto! the Whiskey your Grandfather drank," leave us equally unmoved. Why should we be limited by the tastes of our grandfathers? Besides, we are not sure that Grandfather drank Blotto. And the invitation of a Montreal weekly to "Inspect the handwork of Canadian Peasants" brings Europe to our very doors. Why has no one thought to feature the neighboring New York peasantry in this kindly way? Awake, Salesmanship! and do your office.

The British do these things so much more religiously than we! Who does not remember the exquisite hymn about Beecham's Pills with its persistent undertone of piety? And who that has seen them can forget the old London busses, those Juggernauts of Salesmanship, thickly painted with Lipton's Tea and Somebody's Gin, not to mention Bovril and many another boon and blessing to men?

Mr. Chesterton has spoken coldly of the lunacies of advertisement, but let us rather reflect upon its humors. Close by a vast hotel in Florida, a humbler Boniface has opened his modest inn, accurately described in his publicity as "Next to the largest hotel in the United States." And as a funeral procession moves through the streets of a California city, one reads with rapture upon the windshields of the mourning motors the indomitable slogan, "For a Bigger and a Better Santa Barbara."

Nor must we overlook the musical quality of this material. As you motor toward Perham, eye and ear are captivated by the legend, "Purr into Perham with So-and-So Gas." Or if it be Brainerd, "Breeze into Brainerd" with ditto.

And who has not been stirred by the sublime antiphonies of rival limiteds? "Travel the Scenic Highway through the Allegheny Mountains," is the Alpine call of one. "Take the Water-level route; you can sleep!" is the seductive response of the other. Highland and lowland still forever at war! The higher and the lower path; the drowsy plainsman and the hardy mountaineer.

But even today Salesmanship does not have it all its own way. Now and then a plaintive voice is raised in protest or rebuke. "The dollar you spent yesterday," ominously declares a Kentucky bank, "now belongs to someone else." This is certainly bad news. You did not until now know just what had become of it. Even now you are not perfectly sure the bank is right. The man to whom you—it now appears so thoughtlessly—handed it over has probably paid half of it to some other man for the article he sold you, and he in turn has doubtless paid half of that to the man who sold it to him, and so on down a long avenue of merchants, all nimbly tossing the article one to another for a consideration of 100 per cent a throw, while dimly discerned in the far distance is the producer, apparently a woman, who must have made it out of nothing. Truly, what a thing is a dollar, to keep this extraordinary performance steadily going on!

Perhaps this is too analytical. Strictly speaking, the dollar you spent is now doubtless in the bank—but evidently not in the Kentucky bank which has raised this untimely outcry. Having thus by a little reflection unmasked its perfidious attack upon Salesmanship, let us gaily resume the life of the sellee, to which barn and bill-board, phone, print, and air day and night continually and comfortably invite us.

Let no one suppose that Salesmanship has not its heroes no less renowned than war. Upon being anointed in a barber shop with a peculiarly noxious preparation, smelling strongly of carbolic acid, you venture mildly to inquire of the barber how long you may expect to live. He replies with great vivacity that it is perfectly harmless; in fact, the man who sold it to him drank some of it in his presence to prove it. Most resourceful and heroic of the salesman, certainly, but hardly enough to prove the preparation harmless, without fuller information as to what became of him.

But dead or alive, what a light it throws upon the spirit of Salesmanship! Dashing, debonair fellows, scooting over the highways with their Fords full of samples, they seem lightheartedness itself. But show them a customer, and all is changed. Their sterner qualities emerge, and they are ready for anything; to stand on the lamp shade, or sip the face lotion, or quaff the furniture polish, utterly reckless of consequences, if they but make a sale!

Like those mighty agaves of the desert, that blossom but to die, the salesman who has made his sale has fulfilled his destiny. What more has life for him? Let the carbolic face lotion or the lethal furniture polish do its deadly work. It is upon such sacrifices that Salesmanship moves noisily onward to conquer the world.

Indeed, "By these signs we conquer" piously declares a tailoring company, in a full-page newspaper advertisement.

Not that these heroic men have not like all of us their moments of weakness. I remember one in a western hotel, who, doubtless fore-done with indigestible potations of combustibles or lubricants to convince skeptical customers, leaned over the cigar counter and said wearily to the girl in charge,

"Sometimes I think I'll just end it all. Say, would you care if I did? Honest, now, would you?"

To which, with the most accurate admixture of womanly sympathy and maidenly indifference, she answered,

"Uh-huh."

Publicity is the handmaid of Salesmanship, the salesman's vital breath. From policemen to princesses the modern world is under its spell. Yet one man there is in a prairie schooner in the southwest, who does not own its sway. I called upon him one glorious morning to hold his horses long enough to be photographed. He stopped readily enough but declined the honor.

"Now, brother," said he, "I'd just as lief you

47

didn't take my picture. I knew a case where a man let himself be photographed by a stranger, and that picture was sent back to Montana or Colorado, and it looked like somebody who was wanted there, and so the man got into a sight of trouble. No, I don't want you to take my picture, thank you kindly."

To which his wife added from the driver's seat of the second covered wagon, "That's right! Yuh can't be too careful about having folks take yer picture. Yuh never can tell what they'll do with it!"

How rare is such self-effacement in the thronging life of cities, where publicity plays upon our several senses as on some mighty organ. In a certain ferry-building by the Pacific, the tedium of waiting for the boat may be beguiled by music. "Make the time pass pleasantly," the invitation runs. "Hear the latest selections. Others may be longer but none better." Nearby one is met by the searching query, "Have you smoked a Pessimo to-day?" And farther on, a motion picture in two short reels is in free continuous operation. After watching this through several times over, along with a group of other beneficiaries, you

perceive that they, like yourself, are chiefly occupied in wondering which reel belongs first.
It really makes a good deal of difference to the
story, and you are sorry to embark upon your
ferry leaving the question forever unsettled.

But publicity is not always so pleasurable.
After a long day's motoring you find your lodging in a great hotel, and lie luxuriously down
to sleep. You are immediately aware of a
strange intermittent light flickering in at the
window. You look forth and find that a financial institution, the Lapland Trust Company,
desirous of attracting your attention, has set up
an electric sign facing your window and a quarter of a mile away, timing it to go on and off
every four seconds. The night is hot and you
cannot close the window, but it would be
easier to sleep in a moving picture theater.
And as the Lapland Trust Company patiently
winks you to sleep, you bitterly resolve that
were the whole realm of nature yours, and the
Lapland Trust the only bank in existence, you
would never deposit there. Truly, if this be
salesmanship, then give us death!

Yet for all its famed exuberance, publicity
itself sometimes tires. The happy possessor of

a matchless collection of rattlesnake rattles, in the southwest, modestly described it as having taken a long time to make, "as well as trouble and expense." Evidently danger counts for nothing with this intrepid pioneer who coolly offers rattles at twenty-five cents each, and rattler skins at fifty cents a foot. What a place is Texas! Fear must be utterly unknown, and the deadly rattler, as the novels call him, means no more to them than so much spaghetti. Less in fact, for in a Texas diner I have seen a rugged man wrestling with a plate of spaghetti with look and gesture not unworthy of Laocoon himself.

If publicity is the herald of Salesmanship, science is its acolyte! "Darwin Razors: Motto, Fittest Survive." Science at the chariot wheel of Salesmanship! Or was the salesmanship really Darwin's after all, and was the famous motto just the publicity by which he introduced the salesmanship of his science? Have we then convicted Charles Darwin of salesmanship in which Darwin Limited but follows him, *longo intervallo?* What if ours be but the Silver Age of Salesmanship, the shadow of the golden prime of Darwin, Barnum, and Brigham Young?

One morning soon after these instruments reached our shores, a friend who had been blessed with one, met me.

"I used a Darwin razor this morning" he cried, "and I survived!" I warned him against too hasty inferences, but does this not throw a new light upon the always difficult subject of British humor? Is it wholly lacking, after all, or merely deeper than we have supposed?

The triumph of Salesmanship is written most clearly in its secondary effects upon the language and still more upon the psychology of religion, education, and philanthropy. Everything is now a selling proposition. We must "sell" the cause, the institution, the charity. Our appeal is a "line." The teacher must "sell" instruction. Even the minister must "sell" religion. "The church that's different" is the slogan of a western congregation that has felt the spell.

How promptly have those sensitive plants of our civilization, the universities, responded to this challenge of Salesmanship. The stadium is the store front, and the head salesman is the publicity director. Friday night is sacred to the Pep-session, the laudable purpose of which is to sell the morrow's game to the students. The papers are filled with the deeds, doings, honors, achievements, activities, and performances of the prize professor. The thing that gives charm and significance to all this is that the very institutions that are most assertive in their adoption of Salesmanship and all its works are at the same time setting about limiting their enrolments, thus making it more abundantly plain that there is no purpose in their frantic salesmanship, except the perfectly laudable one of being in fashion. No one can say of them that their manner sorts not with this age, from which they stand apart.

Newspapers estimate their own greatness by the number of inches of advertising they can sell; until now what news they contain is confined to the upper outer corner of the page, where a tiny triangular island of news still lifts its head, not yet engulfed by the rising tide of Salesmanship. On other pages the engulfment is complete.

So also are the magazines. Some demon of display having conceived the idea of interspersing articles with advertising, at the most thrilling moment in narratives of romance or adventure, one is confronted with pills, plasters, tombstones, refrigerators, or radios. If we must have them, why not make them fit? Yet one looks in vain for any effort to arrange the material rationally, or to relate literature to advertising in such a way as to enhance the effect of each. But how glorious to interweave the artistry of salesmanship with that of literature, each illustrating the other! Like that ancient artist who first conceived the idea of painting a statue! Take any of the magazines and spend a winter evening with your friends rearranging it on this principle, and note the improvement.

The trouble is that the acme of Salesmanship is selling you something you do not want. Look about you. Your cook has a lot she does not want. How did she get it? Somebody sold it to her. You take a magazine or two you do not want. Somebody sold them to you, to win a high-school course, or a trip to Europe, or send the minister to Palestine. Thus too many of us become possessed of things we do not and never did want, to the glory of Salesmanship.

A powerful group of financiers is now endeavoring to sell me another house. Learning that I already have one, they have resorted to the extraordinary fiction that I had expressed a wish to sell it, in order to create a demand on my part for another. The matter got as far as the telephone.

"You are wrong," I frantically cried. "I have never even thought of selling."

"Oh yes, you have," reprovingly answered the voice of salesmanship. "We have it on good authority that you wish to sell."

What is the Spanish Inquisition or the Third Degree compared with this? I am still strong, but how much longer can I hope to hold out against the attrition of these assaults? We all know the power of suggestion. In the end, I may become bewildered, contradict myself, lose my temper under withering cross-examination, and find my house sold before I know it, and myself in the market for another!

Must we then prohibit Salesmanship? The attack of the strong salesman, amply backed and highly trained, a practical psychologist, a shrewd economist, with beautiful manners, and the skill of a state's attorney in cross-examination, upon the mere layman, can have but one result. You will buy. No power on earth can save you.

But lest I seem to exaggerate, and since truth is so much stranger than fiction, let me quote from a tract of the great cult that has just been left at my door, by a free school of salesmanship:

"Every day we are all selling something, whether it be merchandise, ideas, or services. Every man has the makings of a salesman in him. I can train you to become a successful salesman."

No doubt he can. But over against this army of trained successful salesmen, what are the prospects of the untrained, unsuccessful public? What about us? Are we just to buy, and buy, and buy, world without end? Or can we devise, if not a free school for it, at least some means of self-protection against this distinctive peril of our day? Some slight technique, at all events, in the way of self-defense, so that we may put up a show of resistance, and at least gain a moment's time for reflection, so as not to be absolutely dumb before the shearer, as it were.

But how idle to talk of schools of salesmanship when we practice it from childhood. An enterprising newspaper has just put before the

children of the City of Destruction an alluring
offer of 50,000 bicycles, skates, and scooters to
be had free, just by getting a few new sub-
scriptions. Three will entitle you to a scooter.
Surely any promising child, still more any puny
or sickly one, should be able to get three sub-
scriptions. Is it not plain that we are born to
salesmanship as the sparks fly upward?

Even our native knight errantry, the Cow-
boys Reunion Association, has felt the spell of
salesmanship, and calls upon you on behalf of
Con and the Boys to help boost the saltiest
Rodeo in the Southwest again this year. Alas!
we cannot doubt that when these centaurs begin to advertise, the end is not far away.

THE COURSE OF BUSINESS

I SOMETIMES wonder whether those affluent persons who gravitate to warm places in the winter and cold places in the summer do not lose something of great worth by these unnatural evasions. Change of climate is of course stimulating and beneficial, but it has occurred to me that its extraordinary blessings may be realized by most of us by the simple art of staying still. Of course, if one lives in Hawaii or some similar place where the climate is, or is reputed to be, stationary, one should travel. But in regions where the thermometer wanders restlessly up and down a register of say one hundred and fifty degrees in a twelve-month, the most blasé system ought to find change enough without migrating.

I remember one bitter winter when blizzard after blizzard swept over us and reduced our stirring city to the peace of a country village. For one never-to-be-forgotten day no motor passed our doors, and the snow was piled seven feet high on what we acknowledge is the busi-

57

est corner in the world. With snow shovels in hand we met in the middle of the street with neighbors we had never known before and shoveled out a road together, so that fire engines and milk wagons at least might come and go. We stayed away from church that Sunday to join with doctors, debutantes, and deacons in shoveling snow, and were not ashamed. As the veritable acme of emergency I would record that a policeman in uniform was seen in broad daylight shoveling a sidewalk not his own. To forestall skeptical comment, I may add that this occurred on the eighteenth day of January, nineteen eighteen, at three o'clock in the afternoon.

But being snow-bound in a great city is not the only beneficial extreme to which one is exposed in the regular course of business. Who that has ever witnessed it can forget the appalling spectacle of a municipal beach in full tide of operation, at the rush hour, as it were? The street-car strike too is something the summer migrant, or should I say vagrant, misses. Who that was fortunate enough to be in town to enjoy it does not remember the great trucks backed up to the curb, with a stout plank for a bench along each side, and a few young women occupying it and trying to look unconscious, while the driver stood by shouting "Twenty five cents to Wilson Avenue! Wilson Avenue twenty five cents!" until he accumulated a cargo. There is also the race war which absentees learn about only through the papers. The summer is clearly no time to leave a great city. It is then only that it shakes off its winter lethargy and really begins to express itself. And above all there is the absorbing interest in the temperature. Will it ever cool off?

Perish the thought that summer is a dull time in town! The very opposite. Freed from the incubus of the upper crust, which has gone to the country, democracy then only in all the year fully comes into its own. The cat's away, and one man is for a month or two as good as another. Our paternal municipality—not for nothing are they called the City Fathers!—organizes pageants and exhibitions for our delectation. There of a summer evening you may wander for hours collecting free samples of breakfast food and soap, or seeing how roller towels and lines of type are produced. The last is most popular, for the new-laid slug is dropped stinging hot into your hand by the jovial distributor, to the quiet enjoyment of forty or fifty decorous pleasure-seekers who are looking on. Of course, if you are a sensible man, careless of public clamor, you drop it on the floor at once. But you do not leave it there. You pick it up and preserve it, for no particular purpose, but from a mere juvenile instinct which the show has reawakened in your bosom. When you went to such shows, you did such things.

A striking feature of the entertainment is a free shampoo parlor conducted upon a lofty dais. You are escorting your only surviving relative in town, and, gallantly desiring to afford her every happiness, you offer her the conspicuous honor. She declines. A gentleman presiding over a stall full of Bibles calls upon you to be saved. You leave, completely rejuvenated. What are the phlegmatic diversions of fashionable climate-hunters to these revels of honest democracy?

These great human experiences of heat and cold are lost by those persons who go in search of so-called equable climates. It may be replied that it is not so much for a change of temperature as for a change of scene that these great solstitial migrations are undertaken. But strange sights too may be seen without leaving home. The excellent newspaper which molds your every thought gladdens your eye of a morning with a group picture of some young men in whom you feel an official interest. They wear a scowling and degenerate mien, their hats are at a threatening angle, and their cheeks bulge with what purports to be plug. The noble old Roman goes on to say that they have formed a most nefarious organization, for the promotion of Manliness in its great typical expressions of Pugilism and Plug-tobacco. Such at least is reported to be the assertion of the president of the new society, significantly named the "Five Minute Eggs."

Distressed at these novel manifestations of culture, you venture to invite this functionary to an interview. In due time you are informed that he is without. It is useless to deny that you experience some slight perturbation at the word. Prince Florizel meeting the president of the Suicide Club comes to your mind. You picture to yourself a hulking ruffian, heavy jowled and sinister, and instinctively loosen your automatic—or at least your fountain pen—in your pocket, when there enters to your astonishment a bright-eyed, apple-cheeked boy, of a completely disarming aspect. You are further disarmed by what this high official of the order reports. It is all a mistake. The Eggs do not exist. They are, so to speak, stuffed eggs. He was going by, and sat in for the picture to oblige a friend who was getting up the group. He was much surprised to see and hear himself in the paper next morning. You understand. Just another joke of that wicked old Roman, who is getting most disreputable in his old age. Let the matter end there.

But it refuses to end. The country still believes the old Roman, and the papers far and wide repeat in awe-struck tones the dreadful tidings of the Eggs. The supposed president receives requests from kindred spirits in distant seats of learning asking for permission to organize local chapters, and full information as to oaths, grips, passwords, and ritual. Grizzled, worldly-wise editors start in their sanctums as the news comes over the wire. They know the signs of the times. A thing may be no bigger than a man's hand, or even a boy's hand, but if it is fraught with meaning, these experienced men will discern it. Editorials both metropolitan and provincial are devoted to the new society. Some of the hornyhanded crew after a column or more of powerful cerebration deem it good. Others just as horny deem it bad. And finally it all goes into the library stacks to guide the future historian of men and manners in our precious age.

But how it shakes our faith in history! Does the famous old Hell-Fire Club of Brasenose College rest on no more secure foundation? We hope so.

I am more and more impressed with the mechanics of society. How intricate yet how constant is the course of business. If a freshman fails to return to his accustomed lodging for a night or two, a nation knows it. If two little girls walking home from school decide to run away for a day or two, and take a job as maids in the next ward, the fact is registered in every daily paper in ten states. Doubtless this is as it should be. The extraordinary thing however is not the solitary exceptional fact, but the colossal background of uniformity of behavior against which it stands out so sharply. It is not

strange that a freshman or a school girl occasionally reacts against monotonous routine.
But it is passing strange that one hundred and
ten million of us live in tranquil and undeviat-
ing conformity with it, doing, broadly speaking, day after day and year after year just what
society expects of us, with a vast and intricate
precision unmatched elsewhere except in the
solar system. No wonder the ancients believed
in astrology.

There have no doubt been times when persons in search of sensations had to seek theirs
in travel. Nowadays we mostly resort to it to
escape them. Yet I would not deny that travel
sometimes has piquancies that rival those of
home. Last summer I hastened through the
scorching heat to catch the Fish Special for my
regular Friday evening journey to the country.
It is scheduled to leave the metropolis at 6:10
but it did not. It lingered idly about the station for fifteen minutes, with all the Fishermen
chafing and fuming at the delay, until a gilded
youth, evidently of enormous importance, for
whom it appeared to have been obligingly
waiting, arrived with a cargo of golf clubs.
This delay also led a mysterious stranger with

a very ordinary satchel to mistake our fashionable and exclusive train for the 6:35 and to pre-
cipitate himself among us.

Embittered by this delay in starting, for I
believe in promptness in trains if in nothing
else, I sought solace in the dining-car, where I
was presently overtaken by a posse of conductors taking tickets. They proposed to retain
the return part of my round-trip ticket, affirm-
ing that the rules of the company required it.
I pointed out with some slight asperity that I
would have no time at five the next morning to
go coursing through the train trying to find the
then custodian of my return ticket. They persisted in their purpose. I warned them of the
dire consequences that might ensue from such
a course, but as these seemed likely to affect
only the passengers, they callously proceeded.
It was the course of business.

Hard upon this second blow of fortune immediately ensued a third. A terrific thunder-
storm came on, which put all the block signals
between Chicago and Milwaukee out of business. We stopped frequently, although we were
not supposed to stop at all, finishing off with
Corliss a few miles short of Milwaukee. Here

the mysterious stranger left us, having learned that he was on the wrong train. The gilded youth remained, and we at length limped into Milwaukee some two hours late.

But mark the workings of providence, intricate yet effectual. At Milwaukee the conductor who had rejected my warnings and entreaties was to give up the train to his successor. The tickets, both one-way and return, which he had taken from the patient passengers, he had deposited in his satchel. This, as is the wont of conductors, he had left on a seat in the smoking car. The mysterious stranger had done likewise, and in leaving the train in great haste at Corliss had taken with him—the conductor's satchel! Judge whether that conductor, when he opened the stranger's bag to hand on his hoard of stubs to conductor number two and descried the scanty inventory of the stranger's travel-accessories, was not a sadder and a wiser man. Did he for one remorseful instant recall my Cassandra warnings? I trust he did.

There was then, I need hardly say, racing and chasing on Cannobie Lea, or wherever Milwaukee is situated, and much telegraphing and telephoning, to trace the stranger and his portentous bag. He indeed carried Caesar and his fortunes. It is doubtful if even the gilded youth's bag would have been so hotly sought for, had the stranger chanced to carry it in his flight. Meanwhile the Pullman conductor in a chastened frame of mind went about the train breaking the news to all the passengers. We were informed that when we were ready to return we might present ourselves at our several stations and on our showing the rich manila slip bearing the name of the company, which the conductor had given us as a receipt for our tickets, we would be transported whithersoever we listed. I began to see that there was something to be said for such a system, after all.

In the end we were only four or five hours late, and, by the time I was ready to return to the haunts of men, the stranger had been located and the tickets (at dreadful cost of collective railway memory, I must believe!) distributed to the stations nearest to their owners' destinations. I marveled at this, for my slip had no mark of any sort upon it. But perhaps that was the way they told that it was mine.

But adventure like happiness must come unsought. We sat the other evening in the peaceful domestic circle when a dazzling flash filled every window about us, and a dull muffled boom sounded in our ears. Various theories at once suggested themselves, to which rumor later added more. Was it thunder, gasoline, or bomb? Nature, accident, or malice? Time at length brought the commonplace solution. A young veteran of the war was entertaining a few youths in his room, which was tastefully hung with the spoils of his campaigns. Among these dusty relics of the past was the essential part of a hand grenade, and to its fuse one of the visitors lightheartedly applied a cigarette, to see if it would fizz. It did. The guests left the room in a body, although it was not time for the basket-ball game. And if we had been wintering in Florida or California we would have missed it all.

At home, moreover, we are most favorably situated for the observation of that most in-interesting of all subjects, Behavior. Take the case of our iceman's horse. This seasoned animal, being strictly regular in his habits, when the dinner hour arrived would set his face inexorably toward home. The iceman thought to mollify him with a nose-bag, but on this particular morning forgot to put it on the wagon. About dinner time as he emerged from a neighbor's where he had left a cake of ice, his horse was nowhere to be seen. Looking up and down the street he descried the rear of his wagon disappearing across the boulevard on its homeward way. The iceman hailed a passing vehicle and went in pursuit. When he reached the boulevard he stopped long enough to ask the policeman why he had not stopped the errant horse. The policeman loudly denied his guilt. He said that the horse on reaching the boulevard had stopped as usual, and looked up and down the drive, before proceeding. This cheerful and intelligent compliance with the law had led the policeman to suppose the horse was going about his legitimate business, and he had let him pass unchallenged. He had not missed the iceman.

What faunal anecdote of tropic climes can claim more human interest than this? Traveled friends may tell of pompanos jumping into the boat at their feet, and pelicans hooking themselves on trolling tackle, but against them all I confidently match this humble idyl of the city streets, the Iceman's Horse and the Policeman.

Even indoor behavior may repay observation. On a certain spring morning the young women who man the outworks of the office brought in word that a Man of Business wished admittance and he presently entered. His hat was in his hand, but the moment the door closed after him, thus cutting off the restraining influences of the gentler sex, he clapped it on his head again, and approached the business of the hour. Could anything be more eloquent? Chivalrous in uncovering before the ladies, with me all artificiality was left aside, and we met as man to man.

The fugitives of climate miss perforce the charms of what may be called Committee Life. You gather about a huge table with a score of people to plan a celebration. The chairman first polls the committee, giving each man's name, or failing that, asking him to give it. Everybody responds cheerfully until the last man is reached. He wears a green rosette in his lapel, and is not pleased when the chairman boggles at his name. "And this," says the chairman, gropingly, "this is—this is—Mr.——."

"Well, who is it?" asks the Rosette belligerently.

The chairman has to own defeat, and the Rosette thus tactfully relieves the palpable tension:

"Now I'm going to tell you so that you'll never forget it again as long as you live." He then divulges the awful mystery in all its portentousness, and the meeting begins. The chairman is a miracle of efficiency. Someone suggests that something be done, perhaps through a committee. The chairman instantly cries out, "The committee is ordered. You are it. Be prepared to report next Wednesday."

A lady enters. All the men but one stop smoking. He continues obtrusively, but plainly without enjoyment. It is evident that with him it is a matter of principle, like keeping one's hat on in an elevator. Upon being interrogated the lady gives her name and says that she represents the Woman's City Club. She is always referred to in the subsequent proceedings as "The lady from the Woman's Club,— I didn't get her name." The lady on each occasion politely repeats her name, and patiently points out that she is not from the Woman's Club but from the Woman's City Club.

Your name is also dispensed with. You are sufficiently described as "The Professor." The chairman inquires:

"What does the Professor think about that?"

It dawns upon you that the lady and yourself do not need names on this occasion, each being the sole representative of his or her species present. You answer for your species and to its name. The high point of the proceedings is reached when the matter of an emblem is up and the Rosette proposes a committee.

"The committee is ordered," cries the chairman in high glee. "You are its chairman. Name your committee, to report next Wednesday."

The Rosette has by now caught the spirit of the occasion. He does not hesitate.

"I appoint the gentleman sitting next to the Professor, and the lady—I did not get her name."

Surely few chance conversations in hotel smoking rooms or on verandas full of bridge can equal in serious interest these committee deliberations.

The greatest adventures, too, are mostly to be found near home. When midway of this mortal life, as Dante put it in another connection, it occurs to you to forsake the proletarian group, and mingle in trade. You have indeed in the War tried your prentice hand at that sort of thing among others, and found yourself conducting a snug little tobacco business for the good of your country. A Distinguished Educator secured for you the ineffable privilege of selling cigarettes without a license, and when you retired from business three months later at the end of the war, your enterprise showed a handsome profit. Not of course for you. Although under a dollar a year engagement, the vast octopus with which you were identified refused to recognize fractional claims, and of course it was understood that you waived the profits. As you do not smoke, and are not eligible for a bonus, the whole affair illustrated the poet's *Sic Vos Non Vobis* on the most complete scale.

The present venture, however, is on your own account, unsupported by academic authority. You should feel some misgivings in this hazard of new fortunes, at the prospect of pitting yourself against the seasoned masters of finance, who might wrest from you your little All. But you do not. Rather, you are buoyant with the hope of coming off with a comfortable slice of their little All, of your own.

The enterprise has been full of promise from the start. There was first the architect. He was all promise. He was the rainbow, appropriately framing the whole bright prospect. Day by day you called upon him for a sketch, and with the unfailing urbanity for which he is distinguished he obligingly promised to get it out that afternoon. One afternoon he did. Your next benefactor was the builder. You never knew anyone so optimistic. Difficulties had no existence for him. In fact, it may be said that time, space, and all other realities fled away at his approach. If you wished anything done, it should be accomplished tomorrow. The brick work would be up by tomorrow night. The roof would be on by Thursday night. The job would be done this week. You feebly observe that the contract has not been signed. You would like to look at it before the building is completed. Nothing easier. He will bring the contract tomorrow night.

The wall is of varying thickness. Some days it is twelve inches, some ten, and some eight. But it always becomes immediately just the size you want it to be. The height of the wall also varies from hour to hour. You can hardly believe that these oscillations will not continue after the building is up, you are in such an Aladdin-like state of mind.

Some contractors are not so. They are timid souls, full of fears and apprehensions, not bright, sunny spirits like your builder. It occurs to you to ask whether he has a building permit. He says he will have it this week; there will not be the slightest difficulty. He will certainly have it before the building is done.

You have a new understanding of what is meant by " good will" in business, and since he simply drenches the enterprise with it, you cheerfully hang out red lanterns over the sand piles on rainy nights, and rearrange the architecture from day to day to accord with your maturing ideas. You do not trouble him with these details. You simply show the workmen where to put the doors and windows, leaving the spiritual values to their roseate principal.

And in the end you leave out nothing more serious than the chimney.

Beyond doubt appreciation is one of the main ingredients in the art of living, and life's richest experiences are generally encountered in the regular course of business. I am not above deriving a passing, and I trust not illicit, pleasure from the observations made to me from time to time by perfect strangers, especially among the young. On the library stairs the first day of college, an eager freshman thrusts his face into yours and thus addresses you, in a tone of entreaty:

"Listen, Sir! Where is the library—the open part, where the students may sit down?" What a world of pathos in his simple words! and how early he has divined what libraries are for.

A very little girl, being led by her mother from the car in which you are riding, stops in front of you long enough to lay her gloved fingers objectively upon your knee, and lifting her eyes to yours to murmur half to herself, "What funny pants!" And you have only time to answer, "Aren't they?" when she is gone. But you hope sometime in the course of business to find her again and to continue a conversation so unconventionally begun.

LANGUAGE, PLEASE!

In Australian barrooms, we are told, when the feast grows loud, the barmaid restores order by rapping sharply upon the bar and crying, "Language, please!"

And no wonder. For language is the symbol of order. When you want to order your ideas, you set them down in writing. Or at least you utter them in speech. This may not indeed at once produce the order you desire, but it is at any rate a step in that direction. A man says to you, "Just let me think aloud for a moment." You know he is struggling to reduce his ideas to order.

It is true that some authors even have minds too completely disordered for the simple device of writing to remedy. Yet there is no other cure. Who has not seen strong men who cannot think effectively without a pencil and a piece of paper? Sometimes a pencil is enough by itself.

Or the professor or lecturer who cannot express himself without a blackboard, even though he put thereon no more than a jumble of meaningless marks? The chalk somehow induces within him an ordering of his ideas and makes it possible for him to speak more or less connectedly.

A candid woman once said to me, "You write too much!" I was more struck with the neatness of the observation than gratified by its personal application. No, we cannot write too much. We may possibly print too much. But the ordering of our ideas, to however slight an extent, that is incident to writing, is real gain.

It is true, a cry like the barmaid's goes up at regular intervals from persons concerned with college English, who see nothing unbecoming in disclosing the less successful efforts of their protégés, over which one might have thought a veil of compassionate sympathy might better have been drawn.

But if we must cherish these critical attitudes, surely there are worthier subjects for them than these. The trouble with such critics is that they read only student efforts. They should broaden their horizon. Why resort to the crabbed and tortuous literature of the undergraduate when in present-day printed books one can read such gems in plain type?

In modern English novels people in idleness or agitation have a disturbing way of "walking backward and forward in the garden." Of course, ennui can reach great depths, and agitation will excuse almost anything, but really, when you come to think about it, walking backward is so difficult and even perilous that it ought not to be resorted to by authors except in great extremities. It bewilders the reader with visions of gardens full of eccentric and weak-minded people backing aimlessly to and fro, and it may be doubted whether it contributes anything of value to the action. Even to fill a spare interval it seems inane. Let the people sit down quietly in the garden, or if they are so full of energy, let them walk around the block, but let them be straightforward about it. We are having too much of this backward school of literature.

Yet actually ennui and agitation have nothing to do with it; witness the incident of the Cornish inn-keeper's wife, "bustling backwards and forwards with various homely dishes," yet, we are assured, "cheerful and full of talk." A perilous business, truly, and all the more so as the author to blame for it is quite oblivious of her danger.

I am satisfied that this is in fact an established British usage, for I have actually encountered an admiral "pacing backwards and forwards on his quarterdeck." It would not be so bad if they first moved forward, but no! They invariably start backward. I can make nothing of it, and if admirals have taken it up, it is the end.

The publishers are not a whit behind the authors in this matter. In a recent book-announcement we read, "Woven into the meat of this book are stories of discovery," to which we can only answer with the Educated Seal, "Woof! Woof!"

And why need we regret the decline of English among our undergraduates when we read such astounding sentences as this, in a standard work of literature like the *Count of Monte Cristo?*

"The *procureur du roi* went out, after having double-locked the door."

Dumas' great masterpiece is full of surprises, but it may be doubted whether anywhere in all its thousand pages there exists a more amazing statement. Indeed above even the supreme achievement of Dantès himself in escaping from the sack under water, I would place this exploit, so modestly narrated, of the ill-fated *procureur du roi*.

Not that we object to an occasional unconventionality in language; on the contrary, we find it most refreshing. For instance when we read in a recent book that "with a slight whooshing sound Mr. Murch drank up his tea," we are exhilarated. This is indeed realism at its best—vigorous, authentic, convincing.

With an irreverence said to be characteristic of our age, college students have of late been venturing to criticize the English even of their instructors—a dreadful commentary upon our degenerate times. And yet the professorial English does sometimes leave something to be desired, and beyond doubt something ought to be done about it.

A whole faculty of humanists recently adopted a tribute to some retiring colleagues, to the effect that the seed they sowed "had sprung up thirty, sixty, and a hundred fold"—

a state of things, so far as I know, contrary to both nature and scripture.

And a reputable dean, in a laudable effort to commend his mother, describes her as endowed "with a mind rarely alert and active." He evidently takes after her, poor fellow.

But speaking of deans, a very Eastern one, recently ascending to the house top, stigmatized as Middle-Western the quaint idiom, "Between you and I."

"Between who?" we might rejoin, with the Prince of Denmark.

Do not deans then know Shakespeare? "There is such a league between my good man and he," should have warned them. But if they never read as far as the *Merry Wives*, how can they have overlooked *The Merchant of Venice*, on which the deans of yore laid such fearful stress:

"All debts are cleared between you and I!"

They are indeed, and with joy and gratitude we welcome William Shakespeare to the Middle West, where it is clear on the highest authority that his English still prevails.

But what, after all, is this business of writing? It is not, or should not be, wholly a manual exercise. We all know people nowadays who actually write their books with their tongues, uttering them into dictaphones with electrical connections.

It is the business of the writer to skim the rising cream of his consciousness, not scooping too deeply into the thinner element below. Or, to change the element, sometimes you are peering into your mind as into a pool, which must be calm if you are to see what is in its depths. This is why, in moments of quiet or silence, thoughts "occur" to you. Relaxation seems to encourage them more than direct exertion does; so often they seem to take us unawares.

And what, in its creative aspect, is the mind? Is it a well, out of which we draw up buckets of thought, one after another? Or a trickling spring or rill, which must be caught as it falls, or it runs away and is lost? Or a climbing vine, with blindly waving tendrils, which must fasten on something if it is to climb?

Or is it a sort of den from which wild, timid creatures that you have never seen occasionally peer, and too often draw back and disappear again into its depths, before you can grasp them and hold them fast? Who has not seen with despair a good idea thus slip back out of his very hands, perhaps never to reappear?

Some minds work slowly. And some writers will not wait for their minds. They insist on rushing ahead with words before the weary and sluggish mind can create anything for them to record. It is not difficult to recognize books produced in this way; numbers of them spring to memory at the mere description. Can nothing be done about this?

It has occurred to me in surveying our growing national literature that not enough is being said, and more ought to be said, in praise of wastebaskets. In expansive moments, in fact, I feel that there should be a great, sweeping, far-reaching campaign for more and bigger wastebaskets. They are doing much, I agree, but how much more they might do. They have but touched the edges of their field. Their larger possibilities are quite unexplored.

I would give all praise to the wastebasket for all that it is and is now doing. At the faculty exchange where my colleagues and I receive what may be termed our official mail, there is close at hand an enormous wastebasket, into which with an easy and practiced professorial gesture most of it immediately goes. Much of it, I feel sure, unopened, the professorial eye having developed a sure sense for distinguishing the wheat from the chaff. It can in an instant tell an envelope containing a check or an invitation to lecture from one to purchase bonds or encyclopedias on the instalment plan. No doubt we all keep too much in the way of correspondence, but the wastebasket is certainly doing its bit, and cannot be blamed for that.

In some recent renovation or other, that faithful *omnium gatherum* of all that is irrelevant in letters, science, and religion, the faculty wastebasket, was temporarily missing, a most disconcerting circumstance. Absent-minded persons and members of the Romance department, in sheer desperation, threw their mail upon the floor, about where the wastebasket had stood. Others stood about uncertainly, fearful of getting the poisonous weeds firmly planted upon them, yet too conscientious to drop them on the sidewalk or behind the radiator. It was an immense relief to have the wastebasket back again after its well-earned holiday. Not till then did academic life resume its full swing.

But much as does even at present find its way into wastebaskets, thus fully and properly reaching the end for which it was created, the broad commanding fact is that not nearly enough does. More should.

To begin with, much that appears in newspapers. Earth has no sadder sight than a car full of commuters, at evening, homeward bound, desperately searching through the evening papers for something worth reading. And yet perhaps a greater pathos should attend those men who late in the afternoon on through trains can be seen patiently exploring the remotest corners of the morning paper on that selfsame search. Truly, Hope Springs eternal in the Human Breast.

It is true, much is printed in these sheets with no pretense of lasting literary worth, but only to beguile the tedium of subway or suburban travel. Much too in the way of news must be hurriedly and summarily treated, if it is to be news, and not just history. All this is commendable in its way. But there is no doubt that journalism does not stop here, but deeply imbeds these praiseworthy matters in a welter of other sorts of thing, which serve no apparent purpose except to make them harder to find.

There may of course be, in the great Universe of Being, existences so parched and famished as to find even the most jejune of such paragraphs refreshing, and I would be the last man to dash the cup of solace from their shrunken lips. I agree that there are diversities of types among us, and that all should be fed. Yet I insist that after the last of us has had his fill, there still remains in every issue of every paper a substantial residuum properly and unmistakably earmarked for the wastebasket.

Then there are those numerous paragraphs of the morning paper that you have previously read in the evening paper, and those in the evening paper that you have read in the morning paper. They'd surely not be missed, and, as it is, give one a maddening sense of going around and around in a circle, with the prophet, as it were, saying in the morning "Would God it were evening!" and in the evening, "Would God it were morning!"

And is there not also a vast body of publication, not daily but weekly and monthly, alluringly front-covered, which passes before us on the news stands and is no more? It is perhaps unkind to begrudge it its little hour of life and color; it is so brief an incident on its unfaltering way—to the wastebasket. Yet the philosophically minded may ask, Was even this slight detour necessary? Should not that beneficent receptacle have ope'd its ponderous if not marble jaws a little sooner to engulf its own?

Crossing Michigan one afternoon on the Twilight Limited, I beheld a little girl playing with her doll. It was in one of those parlor cars named for American women of letters— Harriet Beecher Stowe, Kate Douglas Wiggin, and the rest. They were all that such cars ought to be. The chairs tilted back delightfully, conducing to repose. There were footstools for the feet. The color scheme was harmonious and, if we may still use the word, refined. Nothing had been omitted. And, withal, the illustrious names blazoned on the outsides seemed to permeate the whole train with an indefinable atmosphere of culture.

The little girl, with maternal solicitude based on personal experience, was washing her doll's face with a piece of paper. When this rite, accompanied with much sage but quiet admonition, had been fully accomplished, the child looked about her in perplexity and then said to her mother,

"Where is the wastebasket?"

The whole train seemed to wither at her rebuke. All this magnificence, and that essential forgotten!

FOREIGN LECTURERS

WHEN in the course of human events did people first begin to sit in rows and listen to lectures? This is a point, we believe, of extreme moment in the history of human culture, though little noted by modern social philosophers. With it, beyond doubt, a new stage was reached in what may fairly be called the domestication of man. For it is one thing to sit drowsily by the fireside of an evening listening to the family gossip or wrapped in one's own thoughts, and quite another to assemble with scores of others in a spacious hall and sit quietly by while someone amidst perfect silence discourses more or less entertainingly upon some subject in which you may or may not be interested.

From this it is but a step to the final stage in the process, when one passes directly from one lecture to another. Many active women attend two or three lectures in a single day and sometimes day after day. For short periods and under high pressure, as at Chautauqua, women, and even men, surpass this record. To such persons the term "thirsters" has been aptly applied. They represent the sublimation of the thing.

How did it all begin? Did people commence by instinctively gathering together, and then, to rationalize their action, pounce upon some one of their number and compel him to address them? Or did some compelling personality, with an inward urge toward self-expression, herd them together, to satisfy his yearning for public-speaking? Who can say? For be it understood the problem is not that of religious or political meetings, where you are trying to get people to do or believe something, but of those purely cultural gatherings where no particular course of action is necessarily expected of one's auditors; the thing is done simply for its own sake.

The earliest exponent of the lecturing profession whom I seem to recall was the wily Odysseus. His illustrious biographer also speaks of him as hardy, which was then as now an indispensable element in the make-up of the successful lecturer, if he is to travel far afield without losing his efficiency. And it must be said to his credit that Odysseus did not shrink from long and arduous journeys in his laudable endeavor to fill his numerous speaking engagements and not disappoint his audiences, a thing which all the best exponents of the profession have always abhorred.

As I remember it, Odysseus generally lectured away from home, so that he is the august prototype, not only of lecturers in general, but in particular of the traveling or even the foreign lecturer. Indeed, it was in no small measure the exotic character of his personality, and hence naturally of his remarks, that made him such a success. Think for example of what it means to many a lecturer today to be endowed with a rich Scottish accent! This, or the ancient equivalent of it, Odysseus undoubtedly possessed, and if he was the man we take him for, he made the most of it. Again, like most foreign lecturers today, he had one especially good lecture which never failed to please—an absolutely sure-fire proposition. Like many of our best modern lectures it was largely autobiographical in character, and as time went on it naturally became so extended that it was necessary to give it as a series, or in two parts with a short intermission. The modern analogies of this method hardly need to be pointed out.

Now it is at once apparent that, in this matter of lecturers, we in this country are peculiarly fortunate. In this respect at least we are certainly in the position of the most-favored nation, for not only have we a large native population of lecturers (the *lector Americanus vulgaris* of science) but for some occult reason the lecturers of all other continents and even islands, as soon as they are old enough to accept a fee— the unfailing mark of the adult of the species —make for American shores. As the seals in spring obeying some mysterious inner impulse seek a common goal, so do the great shoals of lecturers with one accord head in the autumn for the American littoral. Nor do they stop there, but in obedience to some obscure instinct, often penetrate far into the interior, lecturing as they go. Indeed, there are well-authenticated instances of lecturers who have in this manner actually eaten their way across the continent, finally emerging at the Valley Hunt Club in Pasadena, or the Bohemian in San Francisco.

Nowhere therefore can the lecturer be so

broadly and objectively studied as here. Who has not heard, right here at home, Italian, French, Danish, Russian, Austrian, German, Belgian, Swiss, English, Irish, and Scottish—above all, Scottish—lecturers? There are also Canadian lecturers and lecturers from South America (Cannon to north of them, cannon to south of them!). Australia or New Zealand now and then uttereth speech, and India, China, or Japan sheweth knowledge.

There was undoubtedly once a time in our history when we in this country produced our own lecturers and were in this respect, as in so many others, self-sufficient. Those were the days of the lyceums, of Artemas Ward, Petroleum V. Nasby, and Mark Twain. Aliens like Charles Dickens seldom penetrated here. But the extraordinary avidity of our people for lectures, once the taste for them had been formed, soon developed out of all proportion to the home supply. It is true the early American lecturer was in a class by himself. He left nothing to be desired. Think of such names as Josh Billings and Ralph Waldo Emerson! But there were not enough of him, and in accordance with the well-known law of supply and demand, lecturers from other lands where there were more lecturers than audiences began to rush into the vacuum.

This was heroic behavior on their part and was effected at no small cost to themselves. Every English novel reveals the blank dismay with which the true Englishman contemplates the prospect of living, even for a limited period, outside of London. Exile is too mild a word for it; it really amounts to being engulfed in oblivion. Further than that, one is cut off from true British food, boiled beef, steamed potatoes, ham and veal pie, and vegetable marrow.

Not only are English lecturers cut off from the delicacies of well-ordered British life, but they are plunged into the perils and difficulties of existence in America. I have seen a seasoned Oxford lecturer stand in positive horror before an American hotel only about as large as all the hotels in Scotland combined, and rail against it. Why? He did not have to live in it; he was staying with me. But some subtle British instinct told him there was not a single wash-hand-stand in the entire building. His whole social background rose up in subconscious protest against it, and all that it implied.

Even this is not all. The foreign lecturer has often to introduce changes and alterations into his lecture before he can give it with full effectiveness all over this country. This may seem a small matter. But Englishmen seldom change. In fact, what they call their "burden" is changing the rest of us to match them. A celebrated Oxford don once lecturing in Chicago paid a glowing tribute to a well-known California philanthropist, who it seemed was entitled to the credit for having brought him there to lecture. He then tactfully paused for a moment to remark that this statement was really meant for his audience in California, where it appeared he had last delivered the lecture. He went on from us to the east, where I have no doubt he continued to praise his California patron, always with the conscientious footnote apprising them that the remark had there at least been appropriate. It is, therefore, no reflection upon these heroic men to say that they are reluctant to change.

But lest we seem ungracious let us hasten to say how great is the debt American lecturers owe this thin red line of reinforcement. French, German, and Italian lecturers might have done something; in fact, they have, but their English is so decidedly continental in character and especially in accent that American audiences still strongly prefer the English and especially the Scottish kind. A gigantic Teutonic sea-lord standing up before an American audience and loudly insisting with every mark of sincerity that he is just a "kit," perplexes our people. It seems improbable, but what if he is? Why make so much of it? Grimm's law is of course what they need, but they can hardly be expected to know it well enough to work it backward. No, the British lecturer may be less picturesque, but we can undoubtedly follow him better.

It is therefore to the British expeditionary lecture force that we owe the preservation of the American species of lecturer. But for their timely arrival he would have died of overwork and disappeared like the bison or the dodo. Consider what they still have to do. One, of my acquaintance, whose efficiency is for various reasons highest in June, once delivered three commencement addresses within twenty-four hours. Of course, as I pointed out to him, even he could not have done such a thing except where the population was extremely dense.

Clearly, the American lecturer is not shirking. He is working at his maximum. But if, as the English modestly put it, he is doing his bit, the American audiences are doing still better. The trouble is our numbers are too small. What we need is 10,000 volunteer lecturers to help meet the insistent demand of our fellow-citizens for more lectures.

It is perfectly true, and I should be the first to admit it, that some of our foreign reinforcements present features that we cannot match. One very brilliant Russian lecturer began by making a tour of the platform, extreme right, extreme left, extreme right, extreme left, never stopping even at the desk where the chairman had originally deposited him. We supposed, indeed, we rather hoped, that after warming up in this way he would steady down and find the desk again. But not at all. He continued to pace swiftly to and fro without a moment's pause for a full hour, when this sentry-go and the lecture came to a simultaneous end. He had walked an even four miles.

A great Swedish explorer is accustomed to

relate to his audiences the unspeakably touch-
ing story of the death in the desert of his faithful and beloved dragoman. When emotion is at
the highest pitch, he throws upon the screen a
picture of the funeral of his lamented friend,
taken at the very instant of interment—thus
showing how even in his loneliness and grief
his sense of responsibility to his lecture audiences did not wholly desert him, and he was
able to control himself sufficiently to slip aside
from his place as chief-mourner long enough to
take the all important picture. It takes a strong
man to be a lecturer: one who can even in times
of utmost stress remember that the lecture platform is his goal, and that far-off future audience
his public.

But strange and exciting as the habits of
other nationals may be, none can surpass in
sheer idiosyncracy the familiar, common, every-
day British lecturer. I know one who when
conversation languishes enlivens the proceedings with a rich guttural grunt—the *ugh* of the
American Indian, uttered in no half-hearted,
casual fashion, but with all the satisfaction,
the conviction, the *empressement*, of Chingach-
gook, Oshkosh, or Powhatan.

Another Oxonian of my acquaintance in his public utterances would invariably preface anything especially good he had to say with an exhilarating sniff; much as Mr. Taft used to signal to the audience that something unusual was coming with his well-known and infectious snicker. Mr. Taft was so far as I know the last among us to practice the snicker. With him it may as an expression of amusement be said to have perished.

One English lecturer used to go about among us wearing a half-length academic gown like nothing known in this country. It was his wont to retreat at intervals to the back of the stage, a distance of four or five feet, and then rush at full speed toward his audience, as though he would hurl himself into their midst, to the great alarm of the front seats, which naturally feared that he might not always check himself in time. But it must be admitted that little devices like this seldom fail to reawaken interest even in the most sodden audiences.

One of the greatest contributions made to the profession by our British confrères is their embodiment of the great ideal of thrift. An especially distinguished one, recently leaving town after an extended stay, complacently remarked that he hadn't paid for a meal while he had been in Chicago; but feelingly added that he supposed they'd all come back on him in London!

Another denizen of the world's metropolis after some weeks in Chicago went so far as to sell his overcoat and even his heavy underwear to his auditors, pointing out to their inexperience the superiority of these sturdy British articles to anything purchasable here.

It must be admitted that these visiting lecturers probably carry back to civilization (as they understand it) many a quaint anecdote from our shores. In the days of man's innocency—that is, before the ladies learned to smoke—a distinguished Englishwoman came to Chicago to lecture. After a luncheon given in her honor, she drew out her cigarette case and offered one of my fellow-townsmen a cigarette. He politely but firmly declined, with these now famous words:

"I make it a rule never to smoke in the presence of ladies."

M. Clemenceau, once visiting Chicago, was

duly introduced by General Dawes and deposited behind the amplifier. As the passion of oratory gradually possessed him, the speaker, like the tiger he was, crept around the corner of the table and became inaudible to the balcony. It evinced its disapproval by clapping continuously, until the indomitable chairman picked up the table and set it once more in front of the speaker. All was again serene until the lecturer forgot himself and again outflanked the instrument. Again our future vice president saved the day, and so on until the edge of the platform was reached and the speaker could no further go.

One of the most delightful experiences of my secretarial life was concerned with the visit to the University of M. Jusserand, then the French ambassador at Washington. It was my duty to meet him at the train, and as I mounted the platform at Englewood, I beheld the ambassador, gracefully grouped with his wife and a policeman before a newspaper camera. The policeman was especially joyful over this, for as he was heard to explain he had been in this country only a few months, and he now had a picture of himself taken with some distinguished people to send back home. As the train pulled out on its way down town all the porters, cooks, and waiters could be seen hanging out of windows and vestibules waving farewells to the ambassador. Here, thought I, is a man who understands democracy, and practices it.

Such was the ambassador's arrival. His departure was no less interesting. It was my duty after his address to offer him the University's very substantial check. He declined it without stopping to look at it. It might have been a fortune! He said he never accepted payment for lectures while he was ambassador. Not a little crestfallen, I informed the President. He shared my gloom. I suggested that we at least purchase his tickets home. He agreed and I got them. All the way to the station, the ambassador kept thrusting upon the President the money for the tickets, which the President good naturedly thrust back upon him. But the ambassador got the last thrust and departed as gaily as he had come.

As the train receded, the President said to me, not without a sense of defeat, "Well, he made me take the money," and handed me eighty-five dollars. "But," said I in dismay, "they only cost eighty." The President laughed despairingly. "Well, what can we do?" "Let's send him the other five dollars," said I. "Very well," said the President, "do it." I did, and received from the ambassador a most amusing letter, closing with the statement that as he had certainly paid eighty-five dollars for his tickets and drawing room from Washington to Chicago, and I had gotten the same accommodations back for eighty, he could only conclude that it was farther from Washington to Chicago than it was from Chicago to Washington.

But many as are the benefits brought us by these birds of passage, they on their part return to their native shores not a little advantaged. Not only can they add to their lecture repertoire a wholly new one on "Six Weeks among the Americans," or "America as I Saw It," pointing out with unerring eye our faults and foibles; but certain intangible values will inevitably cling to them, almost without their knowledge. Thus when Mr. R. Austin Freeman calls his latest hero Mr. Pottermack and then informs you that this is the name of a certain

104

American river, slightly altered in spelling, you at once realize that he has never enjoyed the ineffable benefits of American travel. And how unmusical he must find that historic watchword of ours, "All quiet along the Pottermack!"

LAKE DWELLERS

WHEN summer comes, some trust in mountains and some in oceans, but some turn instinctively and persistently to lakes. History teaches that we cannot understand man's present without some knowledge of his past, and I suppose this yearning for lakes derives from the lake dwellers of prehistoric ages, whose traits persist in some of their descendants, and are brought out by the warm weather.

Some lake dwellers seclude themselves in the sheltered recesses of deep bays; others, more daring, establish themselves on points and headlands. The most adventurous of all push out to islands, and build their houses there, in complete isolation from mankind. An island, said one of our point dwellers, is nature's protest against human oblivion. The islanders underline the protest.

But what sounds are offered the lake dweller's ear! The cawing crows of morning, the croaking frogs of evening, with their perfectly correct "Brek-ek-ek-ek!" still faithful, after

twenty centuries, to Aristophanes. The inde-
fatigable whippoorwill, his piercing whistle
mercifully softened by distance; the owls, with
their derisive "HOO-hoo HOO-hoo HOO!"
with just the rhythm of Cock-a-doodle-doo;
the hoarse croak of the blue heron, the sharp
cry of the kingfisher, and sometimes, far up
some lonely creek, the exquisite call of the
white-throat.

The wild weird rain call of the loon in the
summer night, so different from his foolish
laughter, carries across dark forests and quiet
moonlit lakes for great distances, giving the
listener by his cabin fireside an ineffable sense
of solitude. It is beyond all other sounds the
last word of the wilderness.

Then there are the mellow bells of the little
inns about the lake, calling the fishermen in for
dinner; and in the middle of the night, the
faint irregular tinkle of cowbells far across the
water. On autumn days there is the roar of the
winds through pines and birches, and sometimes at night the tranquil patter of rain upon
the roof not so far above your head. All these
make up our island overture.

These are, it is true, not the only sounds that

break the stillness of the lake. One can remember when the manly shout of the guide or the sportsman was their only interruption. But now the gasoline obbligato is almost continuous. Only yesterday a sympathetic visitor from town was speaking of this:

"Doesn't that sort of thing jar on you fearfully, up here?" he inquired. We admitted that there had been a time, some twenty-five years back, when we felt called upon to disapprove the gas engine, but for the past quarter of a century our main concern had been that no one upon the face of the waters should make more noise than we. There is everything in how you take these little irritations. Adjustment is the constant problem of life.

Then there are the odors—of pine needles under the hot sun, of balsam and cedar; the pungent fragrance of squaw-fern in the August heat; and those strange, sweet scents that come out of the hardwoods at evening.

There are the exquisitely varied odors of wood smoke, birch or pine or spruce or hemlock or balsam or cedar—so different from the odors of burning coal or oil!—floating from friendly chimneys, mixed with the freshness of early morning or the crisp air of evening, and so suggestive of wide, hospitable firesides within.

And then there is that strange faint odor, delicious, yet appalling, which, though never so faintly borne over miles of woods and waters on the night wind, will arouse the lake dweller from the deepest sleep with a start—the odor of forest fire.

Nor must we forget our furry little friends, the native fauna. A neighbor dwelling in the deepest recess of a wooded bay has developed a wide acquaintance with porcupines. After destroying a number of them, he had given up the unequal fight and made friends with them. He had no idea how heartily they reciprocated, however, till, on a recent afternoon as he sat reading on his porch, he heard a scratching at the screen door. He opened it and there stood a handsome specimen of the species and beside her an infant porcupine, black as a coal. She had come to introduce her child.

Even the islander is not without his contacts with wild life. Looking forth from my chamber window one afternoon I was not a little bewildered to see a deer strolling carelessly by.

I rushed out to the dooryard to summon the household, when the deer wandered in among us, very much at home and quite unafraid.

Bent on hospitality, everyone tried to find something the creature would eat; one got a slice of bread, another a carrot, a third some lettuce, but the only thing the deer seemed to care for was a blossoming columbine. Only the kitten held aloof from the general good feeling. Perched upon the roof of his house, he swelled into a black bristling ball and spat vindictively at the oblivious doe. After a decent visit, the deer, pursued by photographers, returned to the lake and continued on her rounds, back to the forester's, where she was staying.

We arrived at the lake one June, to learn that our forest country, after twenty-five years of obscurity, had been pitchforked into fame as a state park—the Northern Forest Park. The change did not as we had feared immediately transform the region into a kind of Coney Island or even Atlantic City, and, except that it was now a bird and game refuge, matters went on much as before.

Except for the beavers. Some enterprising trapper had brought in a few beavers to help

out the muskrats, but they had not become ob-
streperous until this protection system went
into operation, and they came to realize it.
They had before put up a house or a dam here
and there, but now they simply dammed us up
and down. The demon of Big Business possessed them, and in our favorite creek they put
up a dam every fifty feet. They even put one up
between an island and the shore, under the er-
roneous impression that the narrows was a
stream.

For all these extensive works they needed
lumber, and they fell upon the aspens and
brought them down in shoals. There was something almost human about all this sequence:
protection, deforestation, mass production.
Islands offered the easiest transportation facili-
ties, and so they began with them. At the end
of the first season's operations they had cut 110
aspens from the shores of Hikhookmot alone.
I cannot say that this precisely denuded that
island of trees; in fact, one did not miss them
at all. It was the principle of the thing that
concerned us, and so we called in their natural
protectors the foresters and asked the Commission what was to be done. They were all cour-

tesy and regret, and sent a neighboring ranger over to treat with us. We took him around and counted the 110 sorry little stumps, which number he duly verified and noted. He then shook his head sadly over the depredations of his protégés and said, "Well, the little rascals!"

This stern rebuke, thus officially administered, concluded the matter as far as the Commission was concerned.

But enough of natural history. The course of our American life has been accurately reflected in our local social institutions. First came the saloon of old lumbering days, with Mrs. Traurig bare-footed behind the bar, and old Reddy the famous guide roaring down the home road of an evening, brandishing his shotgun. Then came the post-office and general store, at first built out over the lake, so that we all went to it in boats, and waited sociably about the dock for the mail to be distributed. In fact, one hardly had to get out of the boat to get it, and great was our wrath when with the decadence of the times it was removed to a building a few yards up the shore. Getting the mail is not now what it used to be. And then the skating rink, whose democratic scene witnessed the beginnings of many an enduring attachment.

Sometimes, alas! the beginnings only: as when a very personable and adventurous girl, of high literary and journalistic connections, after skating most of a summer evening with a young man of distinguished mien, offered him some maidenly encouragement to call, only to learn that he was the neighbor's butler. Fortunately both of them were able to enjoy the situation, so faithful to the Admirable Crichton.

The rink is now one with Nineveh and Tyre, and its place has been in a measure taken by the inevitable golf club. There it came to pass at a certain tournament that one of the lesser prizes, offered by a popular writer of western melodrama, was one of his own books, duly autographed. It was won by our federal judge, who had read none of them, being so old fashioned as to prefer the exploits of one Nick Carter. When, therefore, the donor asked him to take his choice of all the list, a lesser man might have shown embarrassment. But not the judge.

"I should much prefer," said he, easily assuming the judicial grand manner, "to leave the selection to you, and to have the one of your books which you consider the best."

Few persons now living remember the Rollo books, those excellent and instructive little volumes, written if I remember by the irrepressible Abbotts and full of the most varied information on birds nesting, varnishing pebbles, etc., imparted to the aspiring Rollo by Jonas the gifted hired-man.

I often think of Rollo, but especially of Jonas, as I sit in the study, buried in the woods on a corner of the island, surrounded by treasures of natural and human history that might have baffled them both. For into it are gathered objects of manly interest for which the big house has gradually become too refined; some moose horns, a muscallonge head, silhouettes of our largest fish for three generations, a forked stick used by squaws to push the canoe through the wild rice harvest, old fish rods, relics of lumber days, especially a "peavey" which has launched many a freight car in its time. Against the ceiling should hang, but does not, a lumber sled, with its heavy rusty chains, which we found on the shores of one of our islands and dragged up out of the waves, but left till next season, by which time the ice had borne it who knows where?

Lake dwellers devote a good share of their summer days to fishing. Farming is considered by many a precarious and hazardous industry, but in my opinion it bears no comparison in this regard to fishing. Homer in his more sanguine moments spoke of the fish, "which teeming Amphitrite breeds in countless plenty," but he spoke truer when he called it the barren sea. This admirable remark, which applies equally well to lakes, has often come to my mind as I have sat in the broiling sun with guests from town, waiting for the pike to bite. On one such occasion a local expert, observing us and others similarly unemployed, sculled out to pass the time of day. He offered the usual salute of the profession: How were they biting? We told him.

"Well," he said, sympathizingly, "they don't bite like they ought." He then circled around us for a time, observing our lines and regretfully remarking at intervals, "No, they don't bite like what they ought." We concurred in this, and after some further reflection he summed it all up as follows: "No, they don't bite like what they had ought," and pulled ashore.

Fishermen hold strong views upon the duties of fish. They ought to bite, at least when the wind is right and the sky overcast, it is not thundering, the weather is not too warm, there is a riffle on the water, etc., etc. Indeed, fishermen spend a large part of the summer complaining of what they regard as the unsocial and even immoral habits of the fish in refusing to bite "like they ought." In the intricate social mechanism of the modern world, fish, too, it seems, carefree and irresponsible as they may at first appear, have their responsibilities.

The morning train is styled in bitter irony the Fisherman's Special; though it is to be feared that nowadays it bears more golfers than fishermen in its bosom, in search of the deep peace that is well known to reside in the wilderness.

And there is certainly nothing to equal the tranquillity and quiet the lake dweller may enjoy. Take my cousin Edmund, for instance. Arriving from New York for a hurried vacation, Edmund began at once to overhaul his sea-sled, which had not been in the water for a couple of years. He scraped the paint from her bottom with an axe head, filled her seams with soft putty with his fingers, and finally gave her bottom a coat of green paint. After spending the better part of a day thus employed, he turned her over to put her in the water, and discovered that she was not his sea-sled but his brother-in-law Milward's.

Not a whit disheartened by this disappointment, Edmund turned to the companion sea-sled which was obviously his, and in half a day had her scraped, calked, painted, and in the water. He then put the engine on her stern and set forth to try her out. Well out in the lake the engine for some reason worked loose and flew overboard, in forty feet of water. Edmund instantly took sightings, put down a float to mark the spot, and stood by. His utility man Wally perceiving his plight from his shouts, made ready to grapple the engine out of the deep. Not for nothing had Wally spent five years in a German submarine while the allies swept the bottom for him in vain. Such a sweep Wally now speedily contrived, with a hundred and fifty feet of rope, two boats, and three heavy weights. Twenty minutes use of this device caught the engine from the bottom and brought her up to Edmund's delighted gaze. Even in a submarine life may be lived well.

The north country has a diction of its own. Seeking minnows one day at a general store, we learned that the key to the minnow box was in the hands of the merchant's son-in-law, who was at work on the state house. We instantly envisaged him as far away as Madison, busy upon the capitol, thus rendering his minnows inaccessible. But no! He was not even out of sight, but perched upon a nearby roof from which he obligingly threw down the keys. It was the forester's residence, which is flatteringly described in these regions as the state house.

The summer days pass all too quickly for the lake dwellers, and life moves swiftly with the forest people too. One of them whose husband was in poor health was offered the sympathy of a kind-hearted summer visitor. To which she philosophically replied, "Well, what can you expect? He's no good. He's fifty two!"

Some admirable people, I know, prefer the intimacy and companionship of mainland life, with its stores, its roads, its motors, and its neighborliness. But as for me, give me a good round island, with no fences or gates, no metes or bounds but the deep blue water; with the constant coming and going of boats and launches, purring to and fro, for the mail, the marketing, going fishing, bringing guests for dinner. And in all weathers: fresh June mornings, July lightnings, dreamy Augusts, September gales; velvet midnights, full, tranquil moons, flashing autumn auroras. The islander is a perfect stranger to the commonplace.

THE MAGIC CARPET

Magic is the grandmother of science.

This reflection is forced upon us as we behold the modern scientist flying through the air, darting under the sea, speaking across continents and oceans, and drawing fabulous wealth out of subterranean caverns.

This was just the sort of thing the magician wanted. He dreamed of mastering the world's occult forces and making them do his will. He fancied himself flying swiftly about on the giant roc, entering treasure caves by uttering a magic password; in short having anything he wanted simply by rubbing a magic lamp. Childish fancies, we say; and yet there lurked in them a conviction that behind the visible world lay undreamed-of forces, waiting to serve the man who should learn the secret of their control.

They were right in feeling that far greater powers might and some day would be theirs. They felt that they were greater than they knew.

So let us hear no more of the Vanity of Human Wishes. The Wish *is* Father to the Thought. Most thoughts originate as wishes. We want to have, to do, or to be, and set about thinking how.

Of course, the wizard's mistake was that he did not begin with what he had. He was too quick to grope in the unknown, before he had made the most of the known. He expected to be given what was greatest before he had been faithful in what was least. He had not learned that it is in the commonplace that the utmost magic resides, and that to master the world in any sense, you must first greatly serve it..

I like to trace in the accomplishments of the modern world the fulfilment of those naïve yearnings for unearned wealth and power. The white men who first saw our western prairies thought land that produced no trees would grow no crops, and turned their backs on the garden of God to clear a few sparse acres of the neighboring woods. Others toiled for a lifetime on poor sullen farms, with fortunes in iron, coal, and oil right under their feet. The fertility and the fortunes were quietly waiting for the man who knew; the master of the mighty sleeping jinn shut up in the ground.

As you drive through the flying-fields of Dayton, your thoughts turn to those two Ohio boys who, a quarter of a century ago, set their faces against the whole vast current of human experience, and risked life, fortune, and good repute to win for mankind the mastery of the air. Failure would have just added two more to the long list of cranks, from Daedalus to Darius Green and his flying machine. Success has made the dreams of the old magic commonplace. The jinn of the air like those of the earth, were waiting to serve the masters of the magic secret.

Surely Sindbad the sailor setting forth from Bassorah upon his voyages, in the days of good Haroun al Rashid—which is to say Aaron the Orthodox—experienced no more amazing enchantments than the modern average man daily encounters. He sees men darting like swallows about the sky, or whisking like centaurs over the highways, and far-off voices speak to him out of the night. Someone should write an Eighth Voyage of Sindbad the sailor.

It would certainly be a liberal education in

demonology to cicerone Sindbad through the complexities of modern life. Not that anything would surprise or perplex him. With his perfect confidence in jinn or genii and all their works, nothing would need explanation. As he approached our shores, in the multitudes swimming along the beaches he would at once recognize the mythic mermaids and mermen, whom he had somehow missed on his earlier voyages. Even with them he might almost claim a bowing acquaintance, through his long intimacy with their famous relative the Old Man of the Sea, whom he may be said to have introduced to society. Great ships like the Leviathan would not disturb the discoverer of an inhabited island which turned out to be the back of a live whale. Airplanes would be no more than so many tame rocs flying obediently about, and the subway would be a cheerful place to one who had spent days in the Cavern of the Dead. Towering buildings would be but the magic work of mighty jinn controlled by sorcerers; the faster they went up, the more natural it would be. Rooms that move silently up or down, full of people, would be trifles to one familiar with magic carpets. Fifth Avenue would remind him of the Valley of Diamonds, and if in the deserts of the southwest he saw the loco weed, which maddens those who eat it, he would remember discovering it in the cannibal country on his Fourth Voyage. And as for automobiles, Sindbad would at once perceive that some potent magician, through the use of Solomon's Seal, had forced some sullen jinni to crowd 35 horses all running at full speed under the hood.

For, of course, Sindbad knew that each of these things could be easily done; only he did not himself know how to do it. Which after all is not so different from the attitude of most of us toward them.

Of all the marvelous contrivances of the wizards and magicians of yore, the most engaging has always seemed to me the Magic Carpet. You had but to step upon it to be whisked away with the swiftness of thought—as though thought were always swift!—wherever you, or the sorcerer in charge, desired. You were thus in two places at once, or practically so; now here, now there, as we all somehow yearn to be, our spirits protesting against the limitations of space.

Yet I cannot agree that the brilliant idea of the Magic Carpet was no more than a groping after rapid transit. I see in it something much deeper than that. Its modern analogies are of a subtler complexion. They appertain not to the body but to the mind. You set out for the office of a spring morning with a little modern anthology, which you presently open as you walk and begin to read. It is a harmless little affair, no bigger than your hand, but in a dozen steps it has you in its grip. Everything else is forgotten. You are hundreds of miles away on the flying carpet onto which the jinni you have let out of the book has lured you. You return gasping to find yourself far down the street. There, literally, you come to yourself, amazed to think where you, to all appearances walking down the street, have really been.

Or out of the clamorous overture of *Die Freischuetz*, a sudden celestial melody reaches down and catches you up out of the listening throng, and carries you away among forgotten scenes, and shows you half remembered faces, and fills you with long thoughts of other days —from which, when the music ceases and the conductor makes his bow, you awake as after a long absence, and wonder mildly what has been going on while you have been away.

Before the evening fire of an island cottage a group of eager listeners breathless with interest gathers about a reader, who carries them far away among strange scenes—moors and manors, deserts and oases, south seas and coral islands. As the plot thickens some timid soul raises the cry of Bed! But no! Impossible to leave the magic carpet in full flight; one can only wait till its potent master floats you back again to the starting place.

The magic carpet is undoubtedly a great institution, but we cannot be too careful what sorcerer lures us onto his. It may be the streets of the New Jerusalem to which he will whisk us off; and it may be the sewers of Paris. Who can tell?

But after all, is there not something fairly magical in the mysterious power of those writers who can write to carry us out of ourselves and away to distant scenes, which we realize often more vividly than bodily presence in them could make us, and among strange people whom we presently come to know better than almost any real people we meet? Like the storyteller's carpet, spread in a shady corner of the bazaar, its wizardry seizes any who set foot upon it and whisks them off to other lands. It whirls a whole mining camp away from the camp fire in the western mountains to the London of Dickens and Little Nell. People go about London trying to find the old haunts of heroes and heroines who never lived, and yet are more real today than 999 persons in 1,000. Somebody has created them!

A few years ago I traversed the heated streets of the city of Verona to pay my respects to the tomb of Juliet, whom I have naturally always admired. Of course Juliet never existed, and so the tomb can hardly be regarded as authentic, but we have all been aloft on the Magic Carpet of one William Shakespeare and so we must visit it, whether we will or no.

Not all carpets, of course, are magical. I have begun more than one recent novel and begged someone else to finish it. I recall one in particular in which I had the utmost difficulty in telling the various characters apart, although I usually have no difficulty of that sort. Reading such books is more like dragging a carpet about after you; surely a far less exhilarating experience than being borne aloft upon one.

But what a joy there is in a good book! I read that sentiment stamped on a volume of Stevenson long ago, and it has been with me ever since. Millions of people—more today than ever before—find their chief joy in reading good books; books capable of absorbing their interest and carrying them away on the wings of thought to other scenes and levels. In such books there is a joy quite equal to hearing great music, or witnessing great drama, or visiting strange and distant lands.

Especially I think, when it is shared with some congenial spirits—preferably your household—through the admirable practice of reading aloud, the social way to enjoy a book. Unquestionably it is a greater test of a book to read it aloud than to read it by yourself; but if a book is really good, then I say by all means read it aloud. For one thing, in that way you will really read it all, and be saved from becoming a mere skipper. For another, you will have some one to share the best things in it with, instead of, when you find something really too good to keep, interrupting the quiet of your fireside by bursting out,

"I say, you really must hear this," and then offering it up to them cold, and without its connection, in which invariably half its charm has lain. Upon a real magic carpet there is no skipping about; you ship for the whole voyage or not at all. Sometimes a magic carpet will raise a whole nation of people at once and waft them away in a great common experience. Then we say "Have you read So-and-So? Everybody's reading it."

Few writers weave carpets so big as that. But little or big, the thing must have a power to possess and absorb you; to make you forget your physical surroundings, even to the food upon the plate before you; in a word, to carry you away. In the fine phrase of Sir Philip Sidney,

> A tale which holdeth children from play,
> and old men from the chimney corner.

MY LADY POVERTY

THE American traveler in Europe constantly encounters the flattering notion that all Americans are rich. This is of course not quite true. That we all mean to be rich, would be nearer the truth; and that all of us hope to be rich, would be truer still.

But this is not to be. It must be evident by this time by reason of the low prices of what used to be called securities, and the high prices of what are still known as commodities, that the only hope for the most of us lies in the rediscovery of the beauties of poverty. We have been apostates from her. We must be reconverted. What the times demand is a new St. Francis to preach this gospel to a distracted world. I do not put myself forward as such a preacher. The most I would aspire to is acting perhaps as his Forerunner.

Captious critics may interrupt to call upon us to stand and deliver a definition of poverty and riches, but we reply that these reflections are only for persons mature enough to know the difference. If any reader really does not know being rich from being poor, or cannot tell a rich man from a poor one, this parable is not for him. Even children understand this distinction and begin the categories of perhaps the most familiar of social analyses, "rich man, poor man, beggar man, thief." To be incapable of these elementary social distinctions is to be a moron and with the morons stand. We accept also the distinction between poor man and beggar man; we see no beauty in beggary. The poverty we would defend is that which cannot have nearly all it thinks it wants.

The best approach to the advantages of poverty is doubtless by way of the drawbacks of wealth. Who has not observed the agony endured by wealthy persons who see 50, 65, or even 77 per cent of their comfortable incomes wrung from them by a socialistic state masquerading as the very stronghold of capitalism? Does poverty smart under any greater sense of wrong? Indeed an ingenious Englishman has recently shown that that mythical being the man with an unlimited income would under modern conditions have literally nothing to live on, since he would have to pay an unlimited income tax.

Consider the rich man. Keen rapacious individuals interested in promoting investment and speculation haunt his pathway with designs upon his purse. Meantime charitable people are gathered in groups out in suburban drawing rooms or high up in metropolitan office buildings plotting how to "approach" him. He is a hunted thing, a focus of attack for the inventor and the promoter, the swindler and the philanthropist. No wonder that instead of living in carefree accessibility like you or me he has to be hedged about with mahogany rails, glass partitions, secretaries, clerks, and telephone operators. For he dare not even answer the telephone. He might by so doing be suddenly precipitated into the undesirable presence of one of his natural enemies above mentioned. He cannot know the thrill of curiosity sometimes almost pleasurable with which you and I unhook the receiver.

The rich man has to ride perilously along the crowded street among ponderous trucks and reckless taxis while we walk safely on the solid pavement or ride securely with sixty or eighty of our peers in the intimate social contact of a spacious modern street car, with a coachman and footman—democratically designated as motorman and conductor—to anticipate our every wish. Having sat all the morning in a swivel chair in his office or an easy chair at his club, he now sits on luxurious cushions, the very thing he ought not to do, for it is precisely this continued sedentary life that is throwing him inevitably into the arms of the specialist. It would be far better for him if he were with us in the street car, hanging athletically onto a strap and now and then swaying pleasantly out of the perpendicular. But that expeditious and economical reducing exercise is forever closed to him like answering the telephone.

And this is only the beginning. Consider his distractions. How enormously life's problems are simplified through limitation. Your purse is limited; then so are your problems. You do not have to decide whether you will go to the North Cape or make the Alaska trip or go to Lake George or Palm Beach or Coronado or a dozen other things. If you could really go anywhere absolutely regardless, how hard it would be to choose. And this hardship the rich actually experience.

Nor can wealth so fully rejoice in the simplicity of friendship. It has not the freedom of expression allowed to poverty. For one thing there are the newspapers continually nosing about. Then the rich are oppressed with the apprehension of being used. And the estate of affluence does not invite the social relation of friendship so readily as does the intimate, heroic adventure of poverty. They are moreover constantly belabored by socialists, economists, industrialists, publicists, and fanatics of all kinds, who do not know any of them, or they would have seen what thoroughly inoffensive people most of them are; and all for no earthly reason except that they are rich—for which in most cases they are, of course, in no wise responsible.

What after all is the good of being rich? Suppose you have a wardrobe full of raiment. You can wear but one suit at a time, except in the coldest weather. The possession of scores of others as even Epictetus observed is a purely mental matter. You are pleasantly conscious that you have others, one of which you might have been wearing or may wear another time. But this is a mere state of mind. In point of fact you have on but one costume, just like everybody else. You may even be harassed by the thought that you should have worn one of the others, in which case even the mental balance is against you. Or even that moths or burglars are after them, or that while you are wearing this one the others are going out of style.

There is no denying that some rich people are happy. But does not this disconcerting fact prove upon examination to be explained by their having retained even amid the disadvantages of wealth the point of view of poverty? This is probably why some very rich men down to old age cling to the fiction that they are poor. The honor and the worth of poverty have no more enthusiastic indorsers than the rich. Nowhere are there such firm believers in it as they. They know and do not hesitate to declare that it is good for us. This is not because they do not wish us well but solely because they have experienced, some of them, the sterling worth of being poor. (It is a curious fact that those of them who were never poor are not nearly so certain about this.) What, if anything, do rich men brag about? Not how rich they are but how poor they once were. Caddies tell me that affluent golfers freely dilate to them, in the privacy of the fairway, on how they used to work for fifty cents a day and with what difficulty they got what they call their "start." This striking indorsement of poverty from an unexpected and unprejudiced quarter should convince the most dubious.

The very achievement of wealth, which is its chief distinction, is made from a starting point of poverty, and is itself in reality just one more proof of the worth of being poor. Is it not precisely out of being poor that men grow rich? Human energy, like gas, has to be condensed to be utilized; and poverty is the great condenser. Under its powerful pressure we push, pull, lift, pound, drive, and develop a degree of power of which we did not dream. And in all candor, where had you rather be, in a silken box with the Proconsul, or on scratch in the arena?

Poverty speaks a universal language. Hunger and thirst are alike the world over, and he is to be pitied who has not experienced them in a measure. And, of course, the rich, having most of them been poor, know this and when they

wish to enjoy themselves play at being poor
and strive, by camping or touring, to find hunger, fatigue, and thirst. It is not much fun eating if you are never hungry.

Is it not the simple truth that the rich find
their chief happiness in importing into their
existence the joys of poverty? The competitions
of sport are designed to recover some of the
conditions of poverty. What would sport be if
the richer man always won at golf or tennis?
It is because the decision is sought on terms of
sheer personal prowess, irrespective of Dunn's
or Bradstreet's, that sport attracts the rich as it
does the poor. But this is simply returning to
the conditions of poverty. We have heard much
of aping the rich, but one of the chief enjoy-
ments of wealth may be described as aping the
poor.

But why speak of camping out? In pursuit of
hardship the rich have long since sailed past
that star. The other night a distinguished sol-
dier informed me that there was nothing like a
tent to live in, and the very next day a spirited
woman said with an air of conviction that a
tent was altogether too stuffy a place to sleep
in and the truest happiness was found in a pack

trip through western mountains with nothing
over head at night but stars. Why do the rich
insist upon exchanging the comforts of home
for such conditions? It is because there is a
charm about the conditions of poverty which
even wealth cannot dispense with.

The truth is, we have confused poverty with
something quite different and much more serious—necessity. It is because we think poverty
cannot be escaped from that we dread it. We
are afraid that if we fall into it we cannot get
out again. The fact is, of course, that poverty
is oftener escaped from than wealth. But who
does not dread necessity? It is the *table d'hote*
of life. I remember seeing an English woman
with her son at dinner at the most delightful of
Italian hotels. The dinner was all that anyone
could desire, and it was served with a quiet
dignity that even an American must respect.
But she had brought with her to the table a
large paper bag full of buns, with which she
supplemented the repast. Why? The dinner was
good enough. But it represented necessity,
while the buns symbolized freedom.

We have permitted the novelists, journalists,
and economists to beguile us into the notion

that poverty is all limitation; wealth all freedom. Certainly poverty has its limitation. But is wealth never cautious and timid? Are all radicals rich? Have the great achievers been mostly rich or poor? He can know little of the ways of the world who thinks the poor more sequacious than the rich.

Perhaps you can look back upon crossing the ocean second class. Your luxurious stateroom which you shared with five other votaries of Poverty was situated near the stern and was of a shape unknown to trigonometry, whether plane or spherical. When the stern rose upon a billow, the screw could be heard purring companionably. The five gentlemen who shared these accommodations with you were a farmer, a grocer, a waiter, a Jew, and a probable anarchist. There was no ventilation. But it was a sociable ship's company enough, and when that nadir of the musical cosmos, the Second Cabin Band, was not on duty, it was diverted by two volunteer cornetists, Schnider and his friend. These two did not, perhaps, excel as musicians, but as comedians they fairly qualified. The high point of one of their interminable concerts was the presentation of a superb

cake to Schnider by his friend. At another of
them a magnificent bouquet of paper flowers
had just been presented to Schnider by a blush-
ing admirer with an appropriate solo, when the
captain sent down word that there must be no
more music on deck after ten o'clock while he
was listening for fog horns and sounding his
own. Then the hilarity subsided and you gave
the captain the floor and left the world to
darkness and to him.

Or you may remember traveling third class
on an Italian railway and arriving at Frascati of
an autumn afternoon with your coat neatly
barred across with red from the too freshly
painted slats of the car seat on which you had
been reclining all the way from Rome. Or perhaps best of all you went meandering fourth
class through certain central European coun-
tries now best forgotten. Your train did not
dash madly across the map but moved slowly
and tranquilly, with innumerable stops, thus
enabling you to take in the country with a
thoroughness unknown to more aristocratic
travel. Your fellow-travelers brought with
them for safekeeping their trunks and boxes;
their crates of chickens and their live pigs,

each inclosed, of course, in a stout sack, but easily recognizable by the protests they uttered when their owners picked them up from your feet and slung them indifferently upon their backs. At intervals of the journey your peasant neighbors would open their newspaper parcels and disclose huge sandwiches of black bread and sausage. Upon these they would look long and lovingly, and then tenderly fold them up again, better fortified for the journey from this sure prospect of food. What has first-class travel to offer in frank human sociability to match these memories?

But it would be a mistake to go on and, taking advantage of the reader's overwrought condition, rouse in his breast a positive pity for the rich and a deep but hopeless yearning to do something to relieve their condition. They too have their pride; they do not want our pity. The thing about them, in fact, that I find most wearing is the violence with which they hold their prejudices; but perhaps this is because I hold my own so violently.

A few years ago there lived in the Middle West an energetic and promising young brake-man. He was a steady fellow, and was happily married and had a good home. Unfortunately his father who was a railroad engineer, instead of attending strictly to his duties, became interested in devising some kind of attachment for Pullman cars and produced an invention. The consequence is that his son is now an idle vagrant. He leads a roaming, restless life. His summers he spends at a cottage with seven bathrooms which he has built in the north woods. In the winter he occupies a furnished flat in town, except for an occasional visit to Palm Beach or when he takes his wife north for the hunting season. I cannot learn that he has any occupation. He can hardly be said to have even a home; and all through no fault of his, but simply because his father's mind wandered: a very dangerous habit, most of all in a locomotive engineer.

KEYS TO LOST LOCKS

At lectures before the Royal Society in London, it is said, the president, after introducing the speaker, waits at the door leading to the stage, until the lecture has begun.

This curious and at first somewhat disturbing custom is due to the fact that once, long ago, a timid lecturer, after being duly introduced, was overcome with stage fright, and rushed from the scene, leaving audience and president unedified. Hence the subsequent precaution, enduring even to our days, when lecturers, whatever their weaknesses, can hardly be described as timid.

Upon the death of a near relative I recently became possessed, among other things much more significant, of a key. I had no doubt I knew just what lock it fitted, but when I tried it, it did not work; it was not the key to that lock. I still have the key, but after many efforts I can find no lock to fit it. It is a key without a lock.

Much has, of course, been said of locks with-

out keys; but little, as far as I know, of keys
without locks. And yet what a suggestive
theme it is. I sometimes see before country
churches a horse-block, beautifully surrounded
with green turf; a key without a lock! Or before suburban houses a hitching post, once so
necessary, but now—a key without a lock!
Bridges in remote places still display the old
warning, "Five dollars fine for driving over
this bridge faster than a walk."

I read last summer in a magazine an advertisement of a fishing boat for thirty-eight dollars. I wrote at once for particulars. I was informed that they no longer made that boat, and
I rather wondered why they still advertised it.
Probably it was an old order, unexpired. But
anyway—a key without a lock. There was once
such a boat, of course. In Washington the guide
books call attention to the fascinations of the
Dead Letter Office Museum, with its quaint exhibit of lost letters, so strangely missent. But
it does not exist. Go where it is said to be, and
they will tell you wearily how many times a
day they have to explain that there has been
no such thing for years. A key without a lock!
Of course there was once such a thing, and the

notice of it guided many a tourist to it. But the notice happens to have survived the museum itself.

Of course, this is especially true in the world of thought and of books. So many ideas are offered us, so many courses, studies, formulas, that are keys of forgotten locks. So many slogans, doctrines, mottoes, proverbs—now outgrown. *Poor Richard's Almanac* with its quaint sayings answered well enough for the meager scale and opportunities of Franklin's day, but would never have done for the conquest of a continent.

Who among us has not among his effects a box of old keys—not to be thrown away, for some among them may still be necessary, or become so when some long-forgotten trunk or bag has for a journey in the baggage car to be locked once more. This hope, entertained for the few among them, supports the many and protects them from destruction. Full well do we know that most of them belong to luggage long ago abandoned or doors now shut behind us for the last time. Still we cling to them, unsure whether some of them may not yet prove to have some forgotten function after all. It is so difficult when you sell an old car or turn over an old house to remember to turn in all the keys. So keys accumulate, and many a man otherwise practical enough carries upon his person a weight of metal the purposes of some of which he cannot for the life of him recall—some even which he definitely knows have no more use for him, but only a sentimental interest, to bring back an old house, the old office, some old relationship of which that key is all of a material kind that remains.

For what after all is history or literature but a museum of keys to lost locks? A seasoned friend of mine declares that the whole course of his life from youth to age is faithfully reflected in the keys that still linger upon his key-ring. One little instrument among them was to use in slipping the ring in the bull's nose, for the home of his youth was a Kentucky stock farm. But now—the bulls are gone, the farm is gone, the folks are gone; of it all there remains only this tiny token, a key to a lock that is lost.

Have you ever descended into the nethermost parts of a great library and there in its crypt-like recesses beheld the dead books of other days? Vast areas of dull theologies, forgotten literatures, bleak periodicals, left high and dry by the currents of interest and opinion, out of the stream of common life, discarded and embalmed. Even fiction fares no better than the rest. What is more curious than an old novel? Except for a few great masters, the light literature of former generations is as dead as its science, philosophy, and politics. Only last week a journalist was trying to explain to his readers who William Black was. He could not have labored more diligently had Black been some forgotten Pharaoh, instead of the most fashionable novelist of my youth! How soon we consign them to the remotest stacks, the paradise of the book-worm and the pedant, but to the average man considerably less interesting than a good graveyard.

For here are preserved so many keys to lost locks. Once they served the homely needs of daily life, and opened doors through walls of ignorance, prejudice, and superstition, which no longer shut us in. For this and what we may learn from it we do well to prize them, and keep them, lest we forget the long and difficult path mankind has trodden. Though they be useless as the key to the Bastille, let us preserve and

even revere them a little, for what they sym-
bolize in human struggle and aspiration.

For are we not in effect, all of us, shut in the
innermost recesses of a vast building, out of
whose dungeons we have slowly made our way
first into vaults and cellars slightly more habit-
able, then into upper and larger rooms with
some daylight, and on to really commodious
chambers of size and comfort; yet still locked in
from grander courts and galleries that we somehow know lie beyond awaiting us, could we
but find the keys to open them; and after them
when we find the last key of all, some prodi-
gious out of doors, beyond our present dreams?
No wonder our hands are still full of old keys.

There is in the heart of certain New England
mountains an ancient hostelry, unspoiled by
modern fashion. Its huge drawing room is richly hung with photographs of Boston and Maine
scenery of fifty years ago. Of these it is enough
to say that the ladies in bathing costumes
would appear overdressed for the street today,
while the ladies dressed for the street resemble
nothing at all unless it be arctic explorers in
search of the pole. And yet—let us not deny it
—once we not only respected but positively ad-

mired these get-ups. The more fashionable a thing is in its day, the more grotesque it will afterward appear. And these are the fashion plates of the period.

Instructive as are the pictures in this extraordinary room, they are nothing to its furniture. This is "period" with a vengeance—the period of President Hayes, at its very height. Every piece in the room is a museum piece, and belongs there and nowhere else. No one who has seen it can possibly forget it. But what one yearns for is to see the room crowded with people of that same period: the period of Saratoga Springs and Mammoth Cave; we might almost add, of Niagara Falls, in the days before breakfast-food. But no, the eyes that gazed with satisfaction upon these scenes, the forms that found comfort in this furniture, the hearts that here felt the rapture of luxury and fashion, are no more with us; the locks are gone, and these keys linger thus in out-of-the-way places, presently, inevitably, to be thrown away.

How many old fashions in education, dress, manufacture, and society are such keys. Many parents suffer keenly for trying to bring up children on them. A keen observer recently remarked of a distinguished American politician that his policy was up to date in the seventies and eighties, but he kept on clamoring for it in the first quarter of the twentieth century, a generation after it was outgrown. How fortunate that his career ended in diappointment. For such keys once jammed confidently into new locks will only close them tighter than ever. To know when a key is out of date and to find new ones for the new locks, this is politics. We Americans are confused by the transatlantic fashion of calling the second floor of a house the first, so that the first becomes the ground floor. But is not this because in medieval houses the ground was the floor of the first story, and the first "floor" to be laid with beams and planking was that of the second? An old key, not suited to our locks. And when our British cousins drive on the left, they remind us that when coachmen cracked their whips with glee, it annoyed the foot passengers upon the sidewalks and the coachmen had to take to the other side of the road. But this, of course, is tied up with the origin of right and left drive, and will arouse heated archaeological dispute.

It is said of Old Routh at Oxford, that to the day of his death he persisted in using the stage coach to travel to London, instead of taking advantage of the newly invented railway train. On one occasion when he put down the usual money for his fare, half a crown was returned to him. He asked why, and was told that the fare had been reduced to meet the competition of the railway. Routh pushed back the change. "I have always paid a guinea to ride to London," said he, "and I always will." The old key forever for him. But then he lived to a great age, and once said that he remembered hearing a man tell of having been present at the coronation of the last king of Poland. Longevity puts one to peculiar tests of which most of us have no conception.

In my student days I picked up in Switzerland a five-franc piece of Napoleon First Consul. I presently learned by sad experience that such money does not pass current in Italy, nor in Egypt, nor in Palestine or Greece. I grew somewhat weary of my massive pocket piece, which felt slightly larger and heavier than a silver dollar; especially as it began to occur to me that some designing Swiss had taken advantage of me. But not at all; there were still locks that key would open, even if it was out of fashion elsewhere, for on my return to Switzerland after six months' absence, the wise and prudent Swiss accepted it with alacrity.

Of course, words have been from time immemorial the greatest keys to unlock doors and open caskets and caverns. "Open! Sesame" is but a symbol of thousands of such passwords; indeed in a sense most words are keys admitting us in an instant to a room, a mood, or a vista. At a loss for a word, you feel in all the pockets of memory for it like a man fumbling for a key. And why? Because it is the key to some door before which you stand halted until the magic word is found. Bishop Anderson used to point out in his delightful way the curious experience of the word "Conversation" in the English Bible. From meaning what you do, in the sixteenth century, it had come to mean what you say, in the nineteenth. It had lost its old lock —but it had found a new one.

You stand in a strange city groping for a name—of a hotel, a street, a person. For if you find it, it will open for you doors of hospitality, opportunity, experience. A man affronts you

and irritates you; hot words pass; it comes out
that he is from Boston; knows your wife's
uncle Henry,—magnificent fellow! You say so
too. All is forgiven. You shake hands and are
suddenly friends. A name has been the key to
mutual confidence.

Learned members of Phi Beta Kappa no
longer wind their watches on retiring to rest
with the emblem of that illustrious sodality;
yet there can be little doubt it once served that
purpose, and was expected by the founders thus
nightly to remind its wearers of their devotion
to Philosophia forever. But alas for man's devices! With the advent of the stem winder, the
function disappeared, and now new candidates
for such honors have to be told what the thing
is, or rather was.

Twice every year the City of Destruction is
plastered with posters calling upon the inhabit-
ants to vote for Ryan, Gahan, or Fehan. There
is, it is true, a city ordinance forbidding this
practice, but it is politely relaxed at elections
when some millions of violations of it regularly
occur. I do not rise to complain of this; that
would be futile; but only to point out that after
a certain evening in November they are out of

date—defunct, passé. And still they wave, stained and tattered, for months and even years, clamoring to us to vote for a host of nobodies long since defeated and forgotten—keys to lost locks in the house of Demos, their god.

So many slogans in politics, so many catch words in religion, so many poses in literature, are keys to lost locks. Think of the old proverbs and mottoes that unlocked doors to success and mastery for a former age, but are so useless now. And is anything more pathetic than to see some old fellow fumbling about today with a handful of these old keys? Unless it be to find a young person similarly employed. But what can they do? They have found or inherited these keys, and rightly believe that they were made to fit locks. And some logical people, with an attic full of these keys, naturally conclude that, if there are really no locks any more that they will fit, the thing to do is to make locks to fit the keys.

So we see people busily engaged upon the futile task of making locks for the old keys.

MARTYRS ALL!

THE Age of Miracles is perhaps past, but that of
Martyrs is with us still. Brought up in my
pious youth upon Foxe's *Book of Martyrs* (illustrated edition), I have always realized that
Protestants were persecuted, but only recently
did I learn, from a survey of modern Catholic
preaching, that our Catholic friends feel just
the same way. Whether this is a survival from
the days of Nero and Diocletian, or a modern
adjustment to supposedly Puritan America, I
do not rightly know.

Certainly within the Protestant communion,
the atmosphere is still tinged with persecution
odors, real or imaginary. Episcopalians are
"superior" to Presbyterians, Presbyterians to
Congregationalists, Congregationalists to Uni-
tarians and Baptists, Baptists to Methodists
(or vice versa), and all of them to Holiness
people and the Church of God. And perhaps
this is the place to mention ministers' sons,
who have been cruelly misrepresented in fiction

and literature generally, as I, who am one, should know.

My Quaker friends assure me that misunderstandings with the authorities are not unknown in their religious history; some special instances, indeed, are very vivid in memory unto this day. The Mormons are still keenly conscious of persecution, social if not civil, and even the atheists feel, and doubtless in some places really are, mildly oppressed.

How far this sense of being persecuted is a luxurious inheritance from other and sturdier times, is a question that at once presents itself. At any rate the smoke of persecution still hangs thickly or thinly over our whole religious scene.

But not the religious scene alone. Consider the economic. Has not Labor long been oppressed by Capital? The picturesque idea of Crucifying Labor upon a Cross of Gold certainly had some background. And nowadays Capital in its turn is being more and more pounced upon by patriotic politicians, who need the money so badly. The surtax now being levied upon the ascending levels or brackets is so great that we cry out "Blessed be Nothing,

for it shall not be taken away from us!" Nor is
Capital altogether dumb before its shearer, but,
on the contrary, utters loud outcries under the
stress of Persecution.

Indeed it would be difficult to find a class
now more definitely under the chariot wheels
than the bankers. The legislators at one end
of the rack, and the depositors at the other,
are turning the screws with a will, until—
incredibly enough—we are beginning to feel
sorry for the bankers. As the early Chris-
tians were so persecuted for supposedly having
burned Rome that the Romans began to feel
actually sorry for them (consult your Tacitus),
so now the poor bankers. Perhaps they are
somewhat to blame, but, after all, the fault
isn't wholly theirs.

Not that the politicians have it all their own
way. They too are sometimes reminded that it
is not roses, roses all the way, but the Patriot's
path may be at times a thorny one. In more
than one metropolis they are being rudely assailed, not only by the harmless raillery of the
playful press, but even by the coarser hands of
bailiffs and constables. It has often been observed that no one should qualify as a surgeon

who has not experienced in his own person at least one major operation, and why should not those arch-persecutors, the politicians, have a taste of it themselves? It is not impossible that they may actually be better persecutors in the end because of it.

It must by this time be quite clear that we are a persecuting people, well abreast of Nero, Decius, and Genghis Khan, to say the least. Our eyes once opened to this amazing fact, we begin to perceive Persecution, or at least the persecuted, on every hand. The railroads are terribly persecuted—foiled, baffled, and controlled. They are in fact reduced to positive bondage by the Interstate Commerce Commission, which, it seems, compels them to make bricks without straw, and slays their firstborn generally.

And this is clearly the place to utter a feeble wail on behalf of their hated rivals the motorists. Formerly a free and joyful generation, these are now worn down with manifold exactions. The gasoline tax, originally two cents, has risen to three cents, then to four cents. A gentleman from Oklahoma tells me that in Iowa, he believes it is five cents. No doubt it soon will be; this may be advance information. Six and eight cents are being proposed. The movement seems to be only getting under way.

The state charges you $20 a year on your car, $40 if you have two; the city $20 on each. I look daily for our alderman to propose a modest tax—say $10 per annum—on automobiles operating in our ward. Of course, this is inevitable; it is just a question of who thinks of it first. Smaller places defray their current expenses by arresting opulent-looking travelers by motor who may stray across their miserable precincts. Any pretext will do. Is it not clear that the automobilists are at the present hour perhaps the most bitterly persecuted lot of us all?

But in this headlong listing of oppressed "groups," as it is now proper to call them, we are overlooking the most ancient and time-honored martyrs of all, the agrarians. When have they not been lamenting their miserable lot? Certainly since the Dawn of History, at the very least, and no doubt with very good reason. A distinguished theologian of my acquaintance, once having occasion to spade up the clay soil of his small garden, remarked that it had given him a wholly new conception of the earth's magnitude. But not only must the agrarians wrestle with this gigantic task, but in doing it they are harshly denied such poor compensations as credits, debentures, stabilizations, and the like, which they strongly crave. This inhumanity is shown them, it appears, by bankers and politicians—two groups which, as we have seen, are not without a sense of persecution themselves, in their weak way. But they are mere tyros at it, beside the agrarians, or "farmers," as they are derisively called.

One of these latter of my acquaintance, fordone with persecution, has voluntarily banished himself from the American scene and taken up his solitary abode upon an island of the Pacific, thirty miles from the nearest settlement, and with no human company but the keeper of the lighthouse—as a kind of vast resentful gesture to his oppressors. I can recall nothing like it since Shakespeare.

Of course this sort of thing does not appeal to me. Something less costly and magnificent might make them feel a good deal worse. But it reflects the agrarian complex at its maximum, and says to any scoffers who may deny the whole thing, "There must be a Persecution, for here is a Martyr."

In the literary field, who does not know that, where two or three authors are gathered together, an unfailing topic is the rapacity, avarice, cruelty, and greed of publishers? Some refuse the choicest works (here we point with satisfaction to the immortal incident of R.L.S. and the office boy). Others actually snatch the manuscript, half finished, from our supine fingers. Some charge too much for our works, others too little. "Corrections" too are a source of discord. Sometimes they swallow the royalties up bodily. Formats, blurbs, and jackets are other forms of annoyance. Sometimes without the least warning they change the color of the cover from a soft, seductive rose to a repulsive mouse-color or drab. Flesh and blood can hardly bear the afflictions put upon helpless authors—chief among which is of course that they never sell half as many of our books as they really should.

There is also the whole matter of persecution in education. This ranges from the oppressed schoolboy whom the brutal teacher hits with a cane (see English literature, *passim*) to the

professor who is "relieved" by his capricious
and tyrannical employers for saying the wrong
thing. In some institutions of learning, it is
said, professors suffer grievous persecutions
from the deans—recalling the terrible incident
of the Oxford tutor who was starved to death,
in the tower of New College, in the seventeenth
century, by his Dean!

Even college presidents, who would seem to
have achieved security and calm, if anybody
has, are haunted and hounded by grisly shapes
of trustees, faculty, students, and alumni. One
of the soundest of them, having recently celebrated his retirement from active presidential
life, was heard to express the most boundless
satisfaction at no longer having to give any
heed whatever to these turbulent bodies. No
wonder these excellent men are sometimes
heard demanding, in the experienced tones of
authority, the foremost place in the Army of
Martyrs.

Within the fields of learning, too, Science is,
or was, persecuted by Theology and the Clas-
sics, and now persecutes its greedy little sisters
the Social Sciences, causing them to weep scald-
ing tears.

One is more and more struck in all this by the skilful use made of persecution—not so much by the persecutors as by the persecuted. If you can really show that you are a victim of persecution, you have achieved something. People will rally round you—that is, people of the right sort, who feel persecuted themselves.

On the other hand, if you can make out that somebody is a persecutor, you have him at a serious disadvantage. You have turned the tables on him. He is put on the defensive and may soon be in full retreat. So well recognized is the advantage of the persecuted that even the press, which would seem to have everything its own way, occasionally yearns for it, and may be heard complaining of the loss of its "liberty"! You wonder what it would do if it had it.

And why should I speak of the mutual persecution of Wet and Dry? The "tyranny of drink" is a phrase that tells its own story. But the Wets, awakening to the tactical disadvantage of being cast for the persecutors, have assumed the rôle of martyrs, and now depict the Dry as a savage and brutal Simon Legree, gnashing his whiskers, cracking a whip, and supported by bloodhounds. A crusade has been declared to rescue I know not what holy place from the infidel, and the persecution complex has a new incarnation.

The Pacifist too is a persecuted man. He is vehemently assailed by the press, the admirals, and the Navy League, and finds it difficult to become a citizen of the United States. The Militarist also takes some hard knocks now and then, but in this matter of being persecuted he cannot compare with the Pacifist. The Supreme Court has settled that.

Much reading of the lamentations uttered so abundantly in the "Vox Populi" columns and the like has convinced me that perhaps our most persecuted class is the real-estate owners. It appears that between the janitors and coal-dealers and mortgage-holders on the one hand, and the taxing bodies (of which there are said to be 15,000 in our state) on the other, these unhappy creatures, including myself, will soon be torn limb from limb, and even so will not provide limbs enough to go round. Some of our citizens, being unable to meet these varied exactions, have relinquished their hearths and homes to the state, which is thereby unex-

pectedly set up in business as a landlord, prepared to rent the premises, duly decorated, to
all and sundry. Should which condition become general, it may be hard to tell us pretty
soon from a little bit of the Soviet Republic.

Eminent actors, too, have been heard to say
that the stage is doomed. What with the
movies and the talkies on the one hand, and
the stage hands and the ticket speculators on
the other, they declare, the days of the legitimate drama are numbered.

There is also the innumerable company of
family martyrs, so familiar to us all. And
when it comes to the whole racial complex,
with its superiorities and its rancors, one
can only exclaim with the Apostle, "Who is
sufficient for these things?" The Negro, the
Chinese, the Irishman, the Jew, the Scot, the
Dutchman, the Italian, the Englishman, the
Yankee—one knows not where to end. And yet
we are, all in all, a tolerant and a patient
people.

I do not propose to psychologize about all
this, or to attempt to rationalize it. It may be
in many instances an escape mechanism for the
disappointed. I do not deny that there is a great

deal of truth in some of these attitudes. But it has seemed to me that a broad and rapid survey might help to correct what must often be a morbid state of mind. For I would not of course increase this vast web of misunderstanding; I would allay it.

It must at any rate be clear that there are more martyrs now than ever before. Indeed it seems difficult now to accomplish anything unless you are persecuted or can convince people that you are. The modern position is one thunderous indorsement of the ancient beatitude, "Blessed are the persecuted!" One perceives that numbers of people perfectly well off are trying to make out that they are oppressed. We have reached a point where a majority of our people are martyrs, or claim to be. The persecution complex has become a disease, and more than that, an epidemic. And if there is anything sadder than a persecuted man, it is one who thinks he is, and isn't.

CASSIODORUS

In the figure of Cassiodorus I sometimes find no little comfort and inspiration. In the confusion that ushered out Antiquity, he stands like a tower. Himself a flower of the older culture, he saw the rising tide of the barbarians and the peril in which that culture stood, and after an active official life of great distinction, for he was the minister of Theodoric and his successors, he retired at the age of fifty, and devoted the rest of his long life, some forty-five years, to seeking to perpetuate the old culture he held so dear. He wrote the story of his Gothic masters, gathered and copied manuscripts, and established monasteries to preserve and cherish the old learning in the new barbarian world. For the game was up, and the centuries of Italian supremacy were over.

The beauty of Cassiodorus was that, keenly as he felt this, he did not degenerate or despair. He did not mope or sulk. He exerted himself. He believed in the old culture, and he worked to perpetuate it. He perceived that there were ways to do this and to these ways he gave himself for nearly half a century. His was a great retirement, and he lives in history more for it than for his public life. Let us therefore as we grow old remember Cassiodorus and meditate upon his ways.

For in some respects, it must be admitted, we are not so much better off than Cassiodorus was. In the City of Destruction, we are told, Vandals in the year 1931 damaged public-school buildings to the amount of $334,000, in divers playful ways. Sometimes they set them on fire, sometimes they stole the specie, sometimes they carried off the furniture. In their lighter moments they broke 42,000 panes of glass in them. All at the taxpayers' expense. Broad-minded judges took a genial view of it all. Boys will be boys. And Vandals will be Vandals. If Cassiodorus saw anything worse than this on the horizon, I wonder what it was.

It is said that an early Illinois legislature was persuaded to name the second capital of the state Vandalia because some Indians called Vandals had once occupied that region. Of course the information was not altogether accurate, and yet considered broadly, and as we look back upon it today, there was something to be said for the idea. It was at the worst only premature. In the City of Destruction, for example, motorists are compelled by law to carry on their windshields a large mustard-colored pickle label shaped like a caterpillar, such being the fancy of the City Fathers! We can only rejoice with trembling that such tastes did not prevail when our national emblem was designed.

When as now more buildings are being torn down in our cities than are being put up, we can for a little realize what happened in Rome in the Middle Ages, after the barbarians had had their say for a few hundred years. And when we see the whole front of a stately theater given over to the sale of a five-cent orange drink, we can almost say with the prophet,

> Both screech owl and porcupine
> shall lodge in her capitals.
> The owl shall hoot in the window,
> The bustard on the threshold!

And when our enlightened federal government takes the position that printed pages of Ethiopic are not a foreign language but kabbalistic drawings and are to be taxed accordingly when printed in foreign parts and brought to our shores, it is no wonder so few of us take up Ethiopic as a vocation. So might Hengist and Horsa have regarded a Greek text, had one come to their attention. Once more, the barbarian *redivivus*.

But the misconduct of a few poor urchins is hardly enough to lead a man of today to see visions of barbarian invasion. It is when the Goths and Vandals take possession of the shrines of culture that we may fairly become apprehensive.

When you see a line of crudely colored drawings hanging about trying to look like an "exhibition," and bearing such appropriate titles as "Aw, what's the use!" you think of Cassiodorus. The barbarians in his day viewed with fatigue the art and architecture of the Graeco-Roman world, along with the rest of its culture. They disdained the old disciplines and would have none till they could create their own. And this they did eventually do, in five or six hundred years, sometimes very brilliantly. But for the present it seems clear that many persons are setting up as painters who should never have touched a brush. We ourselves, in childhood, were headed that way, until with a wisdom beyond our years we determined otherwise. But to how few is such foresight and decision vouchsafed.

A friend of mine was recently talking to her architect about furnishing her new house. She expressed a weakness for certain books and pictures.

"Oh," said he, "Books and pictures? You don't want them; they've gone out."

Five years ago I saw in London a very good English play. A year or two later it reached New York and I went again to see it. One fine line of it in particular lingered in my memory, the high point of the play, and I waited eagerly to hear it. But it did not come. It had been removed from the American version. It was too good for us, beyond us, the producer felt.

We hear much about the censorship of plays, and all the bad things they are obliged to leave out. But who makes them leave out the best things, as too good for the American public? This is the kind of censorship I should like to see ventilated.

The truth is, there are two kinds of satisfaction, one momentary, the other lasting. An elaborate electric sign may delight us for a moment or two; but twelve hours spent in its insistent presence would bring us close to madness. A thing of beauty is a joy forever. The failure to distinguish these two kinds of satisfaction is responsible for much so-called disillusionment.

Not that Cassiodorus has great reason for despair or even for discouragement. Education was never more assiduously cultivated or more generally and eagerly sought. Its subject matter was never more frequently or zealously re-examined. We are all constantly being "surveyed" and solicitously asked what percentage of our energy we put into teaching Course 302 as compared for example with that expended upon 344. The fact that you have written a book on 344 and are now writing one upon 302 may possibly have a bearing upon these percentages which statistics do not exhibit. But the good will and real concern back of the inquiry must not escape us.

Last year a publisher announced a sale of three or four hundred popular copyrights, all apparently of American origin, at the rate of twenty for a dollar. A more pitiable mass of stuff was probably never before offered to the book-buying public. That such books exist in type, on paper, shakes one's faith in Gutenberg. Perhaps it would be better, after all, to be illiterate like the Russians, if this is what we are to read. And yet how heartening to observe that he had been unable to sell them as he planned, and was forced by the sheer indifference of his public to dump them at a sacrifice! After all, the American reader is not quite so low and tasteless as some of our publishers suppose.

Even the newspaper critics are beginning to be staggered at the stuff we are offered in books and plays. "Assuming that Mr. Wade is a competent reporter," says one not too squeamish, "the argot of our younger generation" (supposed to represent Harvard, Vassar, Northwestern, etc.) "is as ugly, as soiled as one can imagine a language becoming." Of course, it is not; but Mr. W., for some reason, wishes to make out that it is. For what reason? Simply because he is attempting the modish Vandal pose.

"I didn't believe a word of this play," says a newspaper dramatic critic. "It struck me as being a reprehensible attempt by a lady dramatist to be as flagrant as the law and customs of the land permit. She has deliberately written a tough, unamusing show. I am not inclined to forgive her."

Happy old Cassiodorus! He did not live to see the Goths take up literature. For to destroy standards you could never have created—this is simply the barbarians over again.

The news of Alaric's capture of Rome led Augustine to write *The City of God*, and twenty years later his dying ears heard the Vandals thundering at the gates of Hippo. But Cassiodorus lived. He lived, and true to the deep human instinct of evolution, he adapted himself; the eternal problem, the eternal duty, the eternal achievement. For our wrestling is not against flesh and blood but against dwindling assets, and disappearing dividends, against reduced rentals, salary cuts and lost jobs, against fading ideals and shifting standards.

To the anxious citizen who asks, "Is this revolt?" we answer, "No, Sire! It is Evolution." We will come out of it economically altered, perhaps reduced; but with some new power, some unsuspected capacity, some sounder character developed. This is the way the race has come, and this is the way it must go.

Cassiodorus realized that his present world was not going to be saved his way, and he accepted the fact. But he was so sure of that way that he believed a future generation would come back to it, and he wanted to have its ideals preserved for them to build upon.

Which is just what Erasmus with his humanists afterward did, undoing the work of the barbarians. And the beauty of it was that Erasmus could undo it faster than they had done it.

Cassiodorus would have rejoiced to see his day. And at any rate no one could have said of him, as Louis XIV said to Villeroi to comfort him,

"As we grow old, we lose the habit of success!"

175

THE USES OF ADVERSITY

You must have noticed the opening of our new village aquarium. It was an occasion of the greatest interest. We all felt instinctively that history was being made. Our village doctor, though retired from practice these fifteen years, became so concerned about the manatee, who was not feeling very well, that he on the spot bestowed upon the creature medical advice worth fully a thousand dollars at his ordinary rates, and thus became our first ichthyiatrist.

My own concern for the fish, though no less deep than his, took another form. I was led to reflect upon the fortunate condition in which they now find themselves: sheltered in a magnificent marble temple, reminiscent of Phidias and Pericles; protected from unseasonable changes of temperature and weather; insured ample, wholesome, and regular meals, and safe from the attacks of their natural enemies— kingfishers, otters, and the Izaak Walton League. They are, in short, in the full enjoyment of what is generally understood as Prosperity, and of course, incidentally, that degree of Publicity that usually goes with it. Security, Prosperity, Publicity—all these are theirs. Who could ask more?

They are also as never before in a position to profit by the inestimable benefits of Modern Science. The water in which they live is in perpetual motion, and is constantly filtered and aerated. Anyone who knows the conditions under which the ordinary self-supporting fish exists—the miserable dirty water he has to live in, full of weeds, snags, polliwogs, and algae—will realize what an agreeable change this must be for any decent fish. It is like being elected a life member of a good hotel.

Now consider the condition of one of them if these benefits were suddenly withdrawn. Suppose him plunged once more, after a short railway journey, in the murky depths of his native lake, all his security, prosperity, and publicity taken from him, and himself thrown once more upon his own resources. The extraordinary thing is that most people would consider him happy! All the real benefits he has lost—aesthetic and scientific surroundings, good living conditions, regular meals, and expert medical attendance—they would think of no importance compared to what he has gained, which really amounts only to this: he has got to go to work.

There is a fearful moment in most English novels when the hero, foully defrauded of his rightful inheritance, faces, though perhaps only for a moment, the unbearable prospect of having to go to work. This, next to death, or at least to living out of London, the author most fears for him. That is not quite the American mood. Our present apprehension certainly is rather, Can we hold our job?

For the first time in the lives of any of us, there has been creeping into our thoughts of late a doubt upon what is unquestionably the fundamental axiom of American life—that our best minds are occupied in business. Is it after all barely possible that they are not? I do not say so; I have no desire to prostrate a tottering market. But cross'd as I am with adversity (to adapt the noble Shakespeare), I cannot wholly escape that suspicion. And yet no one would be happier than I to be convinced that it is groundless.

Meanwhile, what of adversity? It is a fine

art. Whether prosperity is one may be doubted, but there is no doubt about adversity. How to take reduction in wealth, influence, prestige—this is a problem to tax the artist within us to the utmost. Observe a man who has never known it and you feel the lack at once. The responsibilities of wealth are much discussed; but what are they to the responsibilities of adversity? Indeed, these latter are so great as to overwhelm most of those who experience them. One trouble with us is that we have forgotten these responsibilities and simply capitulate at once, under the impression that adversity can mean nothing but defeat.

Adversity is also a medicine. Sitting in the crowded restaurant of a great and gay resort, where people do little but sit down to eat and drink and rise up to play, one feels that a few years more of unbroken "prosperity" would have been the ruin of us.

Adversity is also the most social force in the world. Nothing brings people together like it. In its presence men stand shoulder to shoulder against a common enemy. Prosperity divides us; that is the bane of it. Adversity unites us; that is the glory of it. The market is crashing;

your brother comes over. He has been hit too, but he is more concerned about you. Can't he let you have a check? You pooh-pooh the idea; still, on second thoughts you perceive that you might as well take the check. It was not prosperity that sent him to you.

A certain glorious house where you were once lavishly entertained has passed out of the family, you hear; and that charming girl whose wedding you saw celebrated amid such magnificence has gone to work. Well, you admire her all the more, and know that she works with as much zest and spirit as she played with before. You perceive that everybody is cutting down his budget, just as you are cutting yours, and a fellow-feeling steals over you for people you never really took much stock in before.

It is a great help to realize that you are not especially singled out for calamity; without wishing anybody any bad luck, it is nevertheless comforting to think that lots of other people are in the same boat. This is not an unsocial attitude; quite the contrary. The one thing you dread about adversity is that it will cut you off from your kind, and if they are all going along with you, evidently that is not going to happen. You are not going to be isolated; in fact, you are going to be less isolated than ever. Your friends will still be about you, to comfort and annoy. In fact, adversity may bring you closer to them than you have ever been.

And never in a long and eventful married life have you been so heartily commended by your consort as when in a recent hour of economic stress you compassed an unexpected fifty dollars with your bare pen. Never have you been so uplifted as by her unmistakably sincere refrain, muttered at intervals through that memorable morning, "You're a smart man! You're a smart man!" Only a husband of some standing, whose wife may be supposed to have fully explored and perhaps somewhat discounted his powers, can appreciate the full force of such a tribute after more than twenty years of matrimony. You can only say that, as far as you are concerned, that morning fully made up for the so-called depression. You had astonished your wife! Could you have done so in normal and supposedly happier times?

Cautious friends ask you if a certain stock now at 12½ is "good." You reply that you thought so at 25, and still do. You only regret that you perceived its worth so soon. But such is ever the fate of men in advance of their times. Others, wise beyond their day, saw that it was good at 38 and still others at 50. What a mistake it is to seek to rise above the common herd! Let us rather troop unreflectingly along with them, seeking no personal advantage from our superior intelligence. Let us even, in these days of stress, descend into the basements of the marts of trade and there mingle freely with the common herd aforesaid. It seems to know a thing or two after all.

A young friend who is engaged in the manufacture of door and window screens has been feeling the decline in the market for such luxuries. But he also makes a few washboards on the side, and of a sudden a tremendous demand for these appliances has developed. Explain it as you will; the despised washboard, which has been dwindling toward extinction in our modern electrified life, now sells by the hundred dozen. Why? Imagination grapples with the problem. Perhaps people can no longer meet the monthly payments and so are losing their washing machines. It's an ill wind that blows nobody good, and whatever the depression in the screen factory, the washboard plant is for the present a scene of feverish activity. So probably are the washboards.

Such is your own desolation that you resolve to buy something for the country from your favorite mail-order house on the instalment plan. How fortunate that such arrangements can be made, and how advantageous they now appear! The bill is about $100, and it seems you can pay it off quite painlessly at only $8.00 a month! The thing is almost incredible, it is so simple. It shows how easy it is to be poor.

The only thing in the world they require is that they be allowed to add $8.50 to the total, which seems reasonable enough. Though, when you come to foot it up, they are really lending you $8.00 for seventy-eight months, running more or less concurrently; or, to put it another way, they lend you $624 for one month, or $52 for one year; and all for $8.50, or the modest rate of roughly 16½ per cent per annum. But never mind; why be cold-blooded and bankerish about it? It's worth it in these troubled times. Anyway, you order about the the cheapest bathtub in the whole catalogue, and imagine your satisfaction at receiving at once a long letter in reply, with this cheering statement: "You have made an excellent selection in these furnishings, for they are made of very high-quality material, by expert workmen, and assure you long, satisfactory service."

Now, of a surety, fine words and smooth speeches are not for the rich alone; the instalment buyer is not without his proper meed.

A most enjoyable questionnaire, it seems, is to be filled out to accompany your order. Who is your present employer? A certain university. How long have you worked for your present employer? Thirty-two years. What is your weekly pay? It does not come weekly, alas, but it is easily figured. From what source do you expect to make these payments? (This is getting easier and easier.) Name two reputable citizens as references. . . . .

This really is embarrassing. How can you stop at two? If you mention two, are there not others just as reputable who would wonder, if it came to their attention, that you had made such a list and had not included them? It would really have been easier if the blank had asked for ten. Suppose you meet one of the Trustees, for example, and he has seen the list: he will naturally think, though he may not feel like mentioning it, that of the first two reputable citizens of your acquaintance to come to your mind he should have been one. A most invidious question, truly, and if the questionnaire has a flaw, I should find it here. The idea that a list of two would exhaust the number of reputable citizens you know and would take positive pride in referring to is a reflection not so much upon you as upon your fellow-citizens. In fact, it seems to imply that reputable citizens are few, and that it will tax you to name two. Two hundred would be more like it. Why don't they give you a chance to tell them the people you know? You are half inclined to send in a couple of hundred names just of those you simply don't see how you can leave out, but perhaps that would look too much like a list of honorary pallbearers.

Your wife inquires why you bother to fill in all these details. You reply that you enjoy puzzling out the answers and jotting them down. This is, in fact, the very pleasantest part of the instalment plan. Paying cash has no such pleasurable social aspects. You perceive that the company is getting personally interested in you. Here is a specially good one: "How far do you live from the railroad?" What solicitude! They seem to fear that you are going to disappear in the wilderness and lose touch. You have been living up there for thirty-five years, but you have never figured the thing out before. You decide that you live about a mile from the railroad, most of the distance being water. If they mean to look you up, you hope they will not try to walk.

Flowers have been costing a good deal, it seems. Let us then get out that admirable cluster of artificial flowers cunningly wrought of beads, and sent us by our sister in California in years gone by. What a pleasing centerpiece they make upon the dinner table, not overloading the air with a too heavy fragrance, and gratefully reminding us of the substantial economy we are hourly making by the simple and pleasurable expedient of their use. Thus, if nature prove too costly for us, does man resort to art.

Then there is all that stationery, now slightly outmoded, it is true, of a certain society of which you were last year an officer. Why not fling away ambition, as someone has suggested, and use it up, first candidly obliterating your name in the once proper place? Better men than you have done the like before now.

And have you not illustrious precedent in a certain club you lunch at, where the dining-room slips are all conveniently dated 192— unto this day? But do you despise this frugality on the part of the Council and House Committee? No! With a right good will you change the 2 to 3 as you have been doing for some two years, and silently register approval for officers so mindful of the public good. "*O si sic omnia!*" you murmur, in city, county, sanitary district, state, and nation. Then the neighbors would not be in rebellion against the tax bills, and everybody might breathe a bit easier.

One no longer takes pains to tie his necktie so as to conceal the worn spots. Quite the contrary. Why seek to separate ourselves from the common lot of man? Poverty, we now perceive, is honorable in all. There is something almost indecent now about the gay new raiment wherewith we were wont to greet the spring and match her bravery. Let us rather, like our fellows and companions, resume the clothes of yesteryear. What, after all, is dearer than the old hat, the old shoes? Are not these the very symbols of comfort and ease?

The old car, too! No one shall take it from us. On this subject the telephone ringeth but in vain. We will not this spring slow down almost to a stop before a certain show window in Automobile Row and then find a few minutes after reaching home that our number was taken, ourselves looked up at the city hall, and the salesman set upon our track! From such perils we are for the present free. No dallying with stylish models by Fisher or Fleetwood. Let the world go by—though as a matter of fact it doesn't seem at all inclined to do so, but rather seems, if we read the signs of the times aright, to feel in the main just as we do.

The hardest thing to retrench in is books. You recall with pain the days when you could not buy the new books you wanted; you had to borrow them or go without. Must these days return? Well, for a while you can get on with the books you have. There used to be such things as "standard" authors; they must be somewhere about the house. Why not rediscover the values supposed to reside in them?

Perhaps the depression may turn out a good thing for our literary tastes and habits, as well as our figures.

For the jinn who lurked in jars and bottles, ready to obey Sindbad and Aladdin, were nothing to those you have, shut up in books, behind the glass doors of your library. What heroines of enchantment are there, what paladins of romance and adventure, what villains of perfidy and guile!—all cheerfully and amiably ready to emerge and appear whenever you want them. Was there ever such a galaxy? Charlie Chan and the Count of Monte Cristo, Robinson Crusoe and Dr. Thorndike, Sherlock Holmes and the Knight of Ivanhoe, Jeeves and Father Brown. And the ladies! those queens of our hearts—Lossie and Lorna Doone and Miss Dalton and Little Nell. There are villains, too, but their names do not come back to me. (Strange how easily we forget the villains!)

And how approachable and obliging they all are—willing at a moment's notice to emerge from their seclusion and join you for a solitary luncheon, or an evening hour! Myself, I should fear to state how many luncheons I have had, for example, with the Count of Monte Cristo.

What inimitable conversations one can thus enjoy, and delectable thrills and shudders, alarms, hopes, fears, vicissitudes.

And then how simple—relatively—to shut them all up again in the glass-fronted book-case, for a month or a year, or ten years, until you really crave their company again, when out they troop once more, untouched by time, as fascinating and companionable as ever. Though some of them, you must admit, are not so easy to get rid of, once you have let them out, but hang around for an hour or two, or even all the afternoon perhaps. And even then you cram them back into the bookcase with something like a pang.

As a matter of fact, a penetrating intelligence does not live so long with a literary master-piece like the *Count of Monte Cristo* without dis-cerning in it a deep, almost occult, significance. For is not the Count the college student? The Chateau d'If—that is, of course, the Castle of If—is college (and was ever a college better named? "If College!" This is something that even the new educators have never thought of); the course is thirteen years; the Abbe Busoni is the faculty; the governor is the president; and the guards are the deans. We escape or are flung forth at the end of our sentence into the sea of life, weighted with a frightful handicap (the "bullet" at our feet) and shrouded in our professor's sack; unless we have the address to rid ourselves of it at once and strike out for shore. Which if we reach, and can once get to our treasure island, we shall find what our old professor told us immensely useful for the purposes we have been forming all these long, weary years, whether foul or fair.